New Vanguard • 129

British Submarines 1939–45

Innes McCartney • Illustrated by Tony Bryan

First published in Great Britain in 2006 by Osprey Publishing,
Midland House, West Way, Botley, Oxford OX2 0PH, UK
443 Park Avenue South, New York, NY 10016, USA
E-mail: info@ospreypublishing.com

A CIP catalogue record for this book is available from the British Library

ISBN-10: 1 84603 007 2
ISBN-13: 978 1 84603 007 9

Page layout by: Melissa Orrom Swan
Index by Margaret Vaudrey
Typeset in Helvetica Neue and ITC New Baskerville
Originated by PPS Grasmere Ltd, Leeds, UK
Printed in China through Worldprint Ltd.

06 07 08 09 10   10 9 8 7 6 5 4 3 2 1

For a catalogue of all books published by Osprey Military and Aviation
please contact:

NORTH AMERICA
Osprey Direct, c/o Random House Distribution Center, 400 Hahn Road,
Westminster, MD 21157
E-mail: info@ospreydirect.com

ALL OTHER REGIONS
Osprey Direct UK, P.O. Box 140 Wellingborough, Northants, NN8 2FA, UK
E-mail: info@ospreydirect.co.uk

www.ospreypublishing.com

Acknowledgements

I would like to thank all of the staff at the Royal Navy Submarine Museum for
their great help over the years I have studied British submarine conflict. In
particular, Debbie Corner, Curator of Photos, was most helpful in identifying
several little-used images for this book.

Dedication

In all, 3,083 British officers and men were lost in submarines during the war.
It is to them that this book is respectfully dedicated.

Editor's note

All photographs in this book are used by the kind permission of the Royal Navy
Submarine Museum, Gosport, Hampshire, UK.

BRITISH SUBMARINES 1939–45

INTRODUCTION

At the outbreak of hostilities in 1939, the British submarine force numbered 57 boats, exactly the same as the German *Ubootwaffe*. This was not a coincidence, because British policy in the inter-war years had been aimed at limiting the growth of the German force by treaty – Germany could only build in parity to Britain. Yet the policy was not a success, because Germany had the potential to cause much damage (as she did) to Britain's vital merchant marine. By comparison British submarines, by dint of geography and strategy, could not do the same and had commitments around the world in a variety of roles.

International treaties limited the use of submarines in case of war to the 'prize regulations', whereby merchant shipping could not be attacked without warning. In the minds of the Admiralty and British submarine designers this placed a higher emphasis on the use of the submarine against naval targets, which influenced the direction of British submarine design. This focus culminated in the T-Class submarine being able to fire an unprecedented ten torpedoes in one salvo.

A conservative policy for the adoption of newer technologies into submarine design had both advantages and drawbacks. In particular, the slower surface speed and shorter range of some British submarine classes has been blamed on the use of older diesel engine designs, selected for reliability. Conversely, by retaining a simpler torpedo-aiming technique alongside a contact fuse, the British torpedo system did not suffer the paralysing reliability problems that affected both the United States and Germany at the outset of their submarine campaigns.

The training of the all-volunteer submarine force also reflected the foreseen operational role of the submarine. The Commanding Officers Qualifying Course, known as the 'Perisher' course, focused largely on submerged attacks on larger targets. Training in night surface attack was negligible. Commanders were encouraged to fire large spreads of torpedoes, in part to compensate for the simple aiming technique, but also to ensure the destruction of fast-moving and armoured naval vessels. Such training proved to be exceptionally useful in home waters and in the Mediterranean. British submarines were to have significant successes against Axis naval ships, when they appeared. However, as the war progressed, the use of the gun and the employment of unrestricted submarine warfare extended the submarine's role. By the time the

The World War I-era minelayers *L26* and *L27* were among the earliest British submarines to conduct war patrols. They are seen here together in 1940.

campaign in the Far East was properly underway, British submarines had become fully capable multi-role weapons in the hands of highly motivated and experienced operators.

THE S-CLASS SUBMARINE

In the decade following World War I, British submarine designers experimented with a wide range of concepts. Larger 'Fleet' submarines were developed to operate alongside the battlefleet. Also, submarine 'Cruisers' were tested by the major navies of the world, all of whom were attempting to follow the German U-Cruiser designs of 1917–18. Neither the Fleet nor Cruiser concepts lived up to expectations, primarily because top surfaced speed, reliability and endurance could not be brought up to specification.

Britain had ceaselessly called for the banning of submarines by all nations. While some restrictions were achieved at the Washington and London naval conferences, the worsening situation in Europe in the 1920s and 1930s called for the design and construction of a medium-sized patrol submarine capable of operating in the North Sea and the Mediterranean. The S-Class submarine was the result. Initial design problems were corrected throughout the 1930s, so that by the outbreak of World War II, the S-Class submarine was on its way to being a very successful weapon. It went on to become the most numerous class of submarine ever made for the Royal Navy, with 62 being made between 1931 and 1945.

1929 design (Group I)

The first two S-Class submarines, *Swordfish* and *Sturgeon*, were ordered in 1929. *Seahorse* and *Starfish* followed in 1930.

SPECIFICATIONS

Length overall	202ft 2in. (61.62m)
Maximum width	24ft (7.32m)
Surface displacement	735 tons (747 tonnes)
Submerged displacement	935 tons (950 tonnes)
Bhp engines	1,550 (1,154kW)
Surface speed	13.75kt (25.45km/h)
Bhp motors	1,300 (969kW)
Submerged speed	10kt (18.5km/h)
Range	3,700 miles (5,954km) at 10kt (18.5km/h)
Fuel	Diesel 38 tons (39 tonnes)
Submerged endurance	1 hour at 10kt (18.5km/h), 32 hours at 2kt (3.7km/h)
Diving depth	300ft (91.44m);
	Swordfish 250ft (76.2m)
Armament	1 x 3-in. High Angle (HA) gun, 2 x machine guns,
	6 x 21-in. torpedo tubes with six spare torpedoes
Complement	38

The new S-Class boats were to replace the successful H-Class and improve on its performance. Hence, the S-Class was given a heavier torpedo (21in.) and greater speed and endurance, both surfaced and submerged. Fuel was stored internally, with ballast tanks only

The pre-war R-Class HMS *Clyde*'s high speed made it useful for varying roles in all theatres. It is most famous for its fight with three U-boats, but it also hit *Gneisenau* with a torpedo.

on the outer side of the riveted pressure hull. The submarine was divided into six compartments, three of which were fitted with DSEA (Davis Submarine Escape Apparatus) equipment.

The provision of six forward torpedo tubes meant that the pressure hull of the bow compartment had to be oval instead of the ideal circular shape. This weaker shape would impact on maximum diving depth, but gave the S-Class a heavier punch than its enemy counterpart, the Type VII U-boat, which by retaining only four forward tubes maintained a circular cross-section along its entire length.

The early S-Class submarines underwent a number of changes to the gun arrangement. Both *Sturgeon* and *Swordfish* were fitted with a disappearing mounting for the 3-in. gun. This was found to offer no streamlining benefit over a fixed mounting and the later submarines adopted this instead. In 1936, the Royal Navy adopted a specially designed 3-in. submarine gun. The 20cwt (1,061kg) Mk 1 wire-wound 3-in. gun on the Mk 5 mounting became widely used on all small and medium British submarines throughout the war and proved a reliable weapon in service. It could elevate 40 degrees, giving it limited anti-aircraft (AA) capability. The gun could project its $17\frac{1}{2}$lb (7.95kg) shell to a maximum range of 12,500 yards (11,425m). The gun was used to sink smaller craft (and to finish off larger ones) and against targets on shore.

The Admiralty had worked continuously to improve the performance of diesel engines throughout the post-war years. By the time the S-Class was conceived, the improved economy and reliability of diesel propulsion was evident. The S-Class was fitted with twin six-cylinder engines with $14\frac{1}{2}$-in. (36.88cm) diameter cylinders, having an optimum running speed

HMS *Safari* returns home in October 1943. It is flying the heavily embellished Jolly Roger to denote its high success rate.

of 480rpm. A total of 224 batteries stowed under the main deck powered the electric motors. These formed a major part of the overall weight of submarines of this period. In the case of the S-Class, the batteries weighed in at 96 tons (97.5 tonnes).

As was common with new designs, teething troubles occurred with these boats. The internal arrangements tended to be over-complicated and the maintenance of equipment was a concern. Later upgrades eased these problems somewhat.

Diving times of the S-Class were good. From fully buoyant to submerged took around 95 seconds. This could be trimmed to 50 seconds if the boat was at low buoyancy.

1931 design (Group II)

By 1931, the basic S-Class design had proven its worth. However, before more were ordered, the opportunity was taken to modify and upgrade some aspects of the design. Primarily, internal arrangements were simplified and maintenance procedures and routines were made easier. The superstructure forward was lowered and the bow buoyancy tank was removed to reduce yaw (temporary deviation from the submarine's course) when submerged. The overall silhouette was reduced to improve surface stability, which also improved diving times. The 1931 design incorporated two escape chambers, strengthened bulkheads, and a reduction in the number of ballast tanks. Hence, when *Sealion* was launched in 1932, the newer S-Class particulars were as follows:

SPECIFICATIONS

Length overall	208ft 8in. (60.6m)
Maximum width	24ft (7.32m)
Surface displacement	760 tons (772 tonnes)
Submerged displacement	960 tons (975 tonnes)
Bhp engines	1,550 (1,154kW); increased later to 1,900 (1,415kW)
Surface speed	14.5kt (26.83km/h)
Bhp motors	1,300 (969kW)
Submerged speed	10kt (18.5km/h)
Range	3,800 miles (6,115km) at 10kt (18.5km/h)
Fuel	Diesel 40 tons (40.6 tonnes)
Submerged endurance	1 hour at 10kt (18.5km/h), 32 hours at 2kt (3.7km/h)
Diving depth	300ft (91.44m)
Armament	1 x 3-in. HA gun, 2 x machine guns, 6 x 21-in. torpedo tubes with six spare torpedoes
Complement	40

Shark, *Salmon* and *Snapper* were launched in 1933, *Seawolf* in 1934, *Spearfish* and *Sunfish* in 1935 and *Sterlet* in 1936. From *Sunfish* onwards, the diesel output was increased to 1,900bhp (1,416kW) by the addition of two extra cylinders to each engine. For *Salmon* and after, twin motors were fitted to each shaft, which doubled the rate of battery charging. Also the HP compressors were fitted to work off each shaft instead of having their own electric motors. This simplification increased space aft and made for improved accommodation facilities in the after end.

1939 and subsequent War Programme designs (Group III)

The 1939 War Emergency Programme authorized the construction of a further five S-Class submarines: *Safari*, *Sahib*, *Saracen*, *Satyr* and *Sceptre*. After nearly ten years of experience of the S-Class submarine, most of the

The successful HMS *Storm*, painted in camouflage for Far East operations. Under Lt Cdr E. P. Young, DSO, it saw much activity including a gun-action in which it sank four ships.

weaknesses in the design had been eliminated and a worthy and reliable weapons platform had evolved. During the first months of the war, the S-boats proved their worth in the North Sea and were to become the cornerstone of British wartime submarine construction, with another 45 being ordered by the end of the war. They were: *Sea Dog, Sea Nymph, Sea Rover, Seraph, Shakespeare, Sibyl, Sickle, Simoom, Sirdar, Spiteful, Splendid, Sportsman* and *P222* in 1940; *Scotsman, Scythian, Sea Devil, Shalimar, Spark, Spirit, Statesman, Stoic, Stonehenge, Storm, Stratagem, Strongbow, Stubborn, Surf* and *Syrtis* in 1941; *Sea Scout, Selene, Seneschal, Senitel, Sidon, Sleuth, Solent, Spearhead, Sturdy, Stygian, Subtle* and *Supreme* in 1942; and *Saga, Sanguine, Scorcher, Springer* and *Spur* in 1943.

SPECIFICATIONS

Length overall	217ft (66.14m)
Maximum width	28ft 8¾in. (8.76m)
Surface displacement	865 tons (874 tonnes) 1939 orders;
	890 tons (904 tonnes) 1940–41 orders and *Sturdy* and *Stygian*;
	854 tons (868 tonnes) 1942–43 orders
Submerged displacement	990 tons (1,006 tonnes)
Bhp engines	1,900 (1,416kW)
Surface speed	14.5kt (26.83km/h)
Bhp motors	1,300 (969kW)
Submerged speed	9kt (16.65km/h)
Range	6,000 miles (9,656km) at 10kt (18.5km/h) 1939–41 orders;
	7,500 miles (12,070km) at 10kt (18.5km/h) 1942–43 orders
Fuel	Diesel 57 tons (58 tonnes) max 1939 orders, except *Safari* and *Sahib* at 44 tons (44.7 tonnes);
	92 tons (93 tonnes) max 1940–41 orders, except *Scotsman* and *Sea Devil* at 84 tons (85 tonnes);
	84 tons (85 tonnes) max 1942–43 orders, except *Sturdy* and *Stygian* at 92 tons (93 tonnes)
Submerged endurance	120 miles (193.12km) at 3kt (5.55km/h)
Diving depth	300ft (91.44m) 1939–41 orders, except *Scotsman* and *Sea Devil* at 350ft (106.7m);
	350ft (106.7m) 1942–43 orders, except *Sturdy* and *Stygian* at 300ft (91.44m)
Armament (1939–41 orders)	7 x 21-in. torpedo tubes with 13 torpedoes or 12 mines, 1 x 3-in. gun, 1 x 20mm Oerlikon (not fitted to *Sahib* and *Saracen*), 3 x machine guns;
	Safari and *P222*, 6 x 21-in. torpedo tubes with 12 torpedoes or 12 mines, 1 x 3-in. gun, 3 x machine guns;
	Scotsman, Scythian and *Sea Devil*, 6 x 21-in. torpedo tubes with 12 torpedoes or 12 mines, 1 x 4-in. gun, 1 x 20mm Oerlikon, 3 x machine guns
Armament (1942–43 orders)	6 x 21-in. torpedo tubes with 12 torpedoes or 12 mines, 1 x 4-in. gun, 1 x 20mm Oerlikon, 3 x machine guns;
	Sturdy, Stygian and *Subtle*, 7 x 21-in. torpedo tubes with 13 torpedoes or 12 mines, 1 x 3-in. gun, 1 x 20mm Oerlikon, 3 x machine guns
Complement	48

Further modifications were made with twill trunk escape apparatus being fitted in the torpedo room, engine room and after ends.

Earlier vessels of the War Programme continued to be built with the riveted hull on welded T-bar framing. With the advent of a high-quality steel (termed 'S quality'), which possessed the necessary qualities for electrical welding, the later S-boats were constructed with a welded pressure hull, *Scotsman* being the first to be so completed. The welding saved weight, enabling the hull thickness to be increased, which improved the diving depth to 350ft (106.7m). In reality, the crush depth of the welded hull is thought to have been around 600ft (182.88m). The use of all-welded pressure hulls had an added benefit, in that the submarines could now withstand a higher level of punishment when submerged. The move to welded hulls was by no means an easy one because of the high standard of welding needed, but its adoption was a great success for the shipbuilders and a genuine leap forward in submarine construction, albeit several years behind Germany. *Stubborn* was driven deeper than 500ft (152.4m) off Trondheim in 1944 and survived, a testament to the quality of its hull. In 1945 in the Malacca Straits, *Strongbow* was to endure one of the longest depth-charge attacks against a British submarine. It was heavily damaged, but survived.

In 1941, with future operations in the Far East in mind, the endurance of the S-Class began to be improved. By converting parts of the main tanks to fuel storage, 22 tons (22.4 tonnes) of extra diesel could be carried. In the riveted-hull boats, further modifications allowed for a total of 92 tons (93 tonnes) to be carried, giving a range of 8,000 miles (12,874km) at 10kt (18.5km/h). The welded-hull boats were more complicated to rework and hence total fuel stowage could only be increased to 85 tons (86 tonnes), giving a range of 7,500 miles (12,070km) at 10kt (18.5km/h).

Patrols in the Far East necessitated further modifications due to the heat and humidity encountered. Extra fresh water and lubrication had to be carried. Also two freon atmosphere control units were fitted in place of the older low-pressure blower.

In July 1941, the installation of an external stern torpedo tube was approved. This could not be reloaded. From 1940 onwards the S-Class submarines were adapted for the laying of mines via the internal torpedo tubes in a similar arrangement to the T-Class. Eight mines were carried instead of the spare torpedoes, with four mines being carried in the torpedo tubes. The all-welded vessels were fitted with the 4-in. submarine gun that packed a greater punch than the earlier 3-in. version. On these submarines, the stern tube had to be sacrificed in order to maintain stability and to save weight.

During war service it was established that the closed bridge, which had been a feature of the peacetime S-boats and some of the earlier war builds, was inferior to the open bridge. Therefore, all were modified to the open arrangement and it was adopted for all future construction.

As the war progressed, new technologies were continually incorporated into existing boats. The cramped nature of the S-Class interior made the fitting of improved attack equipment and radar a difficult job. Both the radio room and control room had to be extensively modified to accommodate the latest equipment.

THE T-CLASS SUBMARINE

With the imposition of tonnage limitations on patrol submarines laid down at the 1930 London Naval Conference, the replacement design for the obsolete O-, P- and R-classes required a new approach to the design of the longer-range British submarine. Surface speed and range

The successful HMS *Torbay* in Barry in 1945. Note the upward-folded forward hydroplanes and the absence of forward external torpedo doors.

could not be expected to match that of the O-, P- and R-Class submarines. Furthermore, because the 1930 conference imposed the prize rules of World War I on submarine operations, the Admiralty looked to its future submarines to be operated as minelayers, in reconnaissance roles and as anti-warship vessels. The future role of patrol submarines in the anti-merchant-ship role was of secondary priority. This perspective had a profound effect on the way in which the T-Class concept evolved. The ongoing development of better anti-submarine weaponry, coupled with the development of Asdic (a sonar device, named after the Anti-Submarine Detection Investigation Committee, who developed it), meant that in the anti-warship role the submarine would need to expend its torpedoes at greater ranges. In order to increase the possibility of a hit, the T-Class came into existence with ten forward-facing torpedo tubes. Such a powerful attacking potential was unprecedented.

The first T-Class submarines were ordered in 1935. Simplicity and reliability in service were given high priority, possibly as a result of what had been learnt during the development of the S-Class. However, the tragic sinking of *Thetis* in Liverpool Bay in 1939, in which 100 men died, pointed to a number of design defects which, when corrected, honed the T-Class submarine into a fine and reliable weapons system.

The T-Class served with great distinction in all theatres of the war and a total of 53 were built. In the Mediterranean, where half of the vessels deployed were sunk, the heroism displayed by commanders of the impressive T-boats won them four Victoria Crosses. Names like *Torbay*, *Thrasher* and *Turbulent* are legendary in the submarine service. Later, *Tantalus* was to make the longest British submarine patrol of the war.

1935 design (Group I)

A total of 15 T-Class submarines were ordered before World War II: *Triton* in 1935; *Thetis* (later *Thunderbolt*), *Tribune*, *Trident* and *Triumph* in 1936; *Taku*, *Tarpon*, *Thistle*, *Tigris*, *Triad*, *Truant* and *Tuna* in 1937; and *Talisman*, *Tetrach* and *Torbay* in 1938.

HMS *Truant* in Holy Loch in 1943. Note the forward-firing external torpedo tubes. *Truant* was a successful boat, serving in all three major theatres. Appropriately perhaps, it was adopted by the submariners' hometown of Gosport.

SPECIFICATIONS

Length overall	275ft (83.822m); *Triton* 277ft (84.43m)
Maximum width	26ft (7.92m)
Surface displacement	1,300 tons (1,321 tonnes)
Submerged displacement	1,595 tons (1,621 tonnes)
Bhp engines	2,500 (1,863kW)
Surface speed	15.25kt (28.22km/h)
Bhp motors	1,450 (1,080kW)
Submerged speed	9kt (16.66km/h)
Range	8,000 miles (12,874km) at 10kt (18.5km/h); *Torbay* and *Trident* later 11,000 miles (17,702km) at 10kt (18.5km/h)
Fuel	Diesel 132 tons (134 tonnes); *Torbay* and *Trident* later adapted to 178 tons (181 tonnes)
Submerged endurance	1.5 hours at 9kt (16.66km/h), 55 hours at 2.5kt (4.63km/h)
Diving depth	300ft (91.44m)
Armament	10 x 21-in. torpedo tubes (six internal bow, two external bow, two external amidships) with 16 torpedoes, 1 x 4-in. gun, 3 x machine guns; *Thunderbolt* and *Triumph* did not carry the two amidships torpedo tubes; In 1942 *Taku*, *Thunderbolt*, *Tigris*, *Torbay*, *Tribune*, *Trident*, *Truant* and *Tuna* were modified to carry 1 x 21-in. torpedo tube aft and 1 x 20mm Oerlikon
Complement	56

The hull design was a welded frame with riveted pressure hull. Saddle-ballast tanks sat outside the pressure hull and all fuel was stored internally. *Trident* and *Torbay* were later altered to carry fuel externally as well, increasing their range to 11,000 miles (17,702km) at 10kt (18.5km/h).

As part of the 1938 build programme, *Torbay*, *Talisman* and *Tetrach* were adapted to carry mines in vertical chutes fitted through the external ballast tanks, in a similar style to that used in the L-Class. The consequent trials with this design proved to be unsatisfactory. The drag caused by the chutes reduced surface speed by 1.5kt (2.78km/h). The empty chutes could be blanked when not in use, but this required the submarine to be dry-docked, using up sparse dry-docking resources. The design was therefore abandoned and the three submarines reverted to their original designs. However, the need for a minelaying capability remained. This was solved during 1941 by the adoption of a minelaying system utilizing the internal torpedo tubes.

With two external torpedo tubes on the bow, the bow wave when running on the surface gave cause for concern, so *Triumph* and *Thunderbolt* were modified by having the tubes shifted 7ft (2.34m) back along the upper casing, which was also narrowed. This modification also assisted in improved depth keeping and was adopted by later builds during the war. As with the S-Class, the enclosed bridge fitted to some was removed and an open bridge was favoured, albeit with increased spray deflection.

HMS *Trenchant* showing its aft-facing external tubes amidships and on the stern. This submarine claimed the cruiser *Ashigara* in 1945.

An early T-Class, HMS *Triumph*, luckily escaped destruction after being mined in the North Sea in December 1939. It is thought to have been lost to a mine in the Mediterranean two years later.

The fitting of ten forward-facing torpedo tubes to ensure greater success against warship targets was a remarkable feature of this class. Six of the tubes were internal and could be reloaded, with one spare carried for each tube. Two external tubes were situated on the bow and two amidships at 7.5 degrees, offset with the torpedoes angled to fire forward. The primary weakness of this design was the lack of a stern tube to be used for defence when under pursuit. In 1942, the surviving boats of the pre-war programme, *Taku, Thunderbolt, Tigris, Torbay, Tribune, Trident, Truant* and *Tuna*, were retrofitted with a stern tube. They were also fitted with a 20mm Oerlikon gun for better defence from air attack and were modified to carry mines that were deployed through the internal torpedo tubes.

The surface speed of all the S-, T- and U-classes in World War II was poor in comparison to their German counterparts. This was in part due to a conservative approach to new innovations and a deliberate strategy of choosing reliability over performance. The O-, P- and R-classes were faster but proved to be too unreliable. Nevertheless, with the construction of the T-Class the Admiralty experimented with diesel engines manufactured by Vickers, Admiralty pattern, MAN and Sulzer. Three hundred and thirty-six battery cells weighing in at 150 tons (173 tonnes) provided underwater propulsion.

1939 War Programme design (Group II)

The seven boats ordered in 1939 formed a transitory design group before the final specification for the T-Class was established in 1940. They were *Tempest, Thorn, Thrasher, Traveller, Trooper, Trusty* and *Turbulent* and they began to enter service in late 1941.

SPECIFICATIONS

Length overall	274ft (83.52m)
Maximum width	26ft 7in. (8.1m)
Surface displacement	1,327 tons (1,348 tonnes)
Submerged displacement	1,571 tons (1,596 tonnes)
Bhp engines	2,500 (1,863kW)
Surface speed	15.25kt (28.22km/h)
Bhp motors	1,450 (1,080kW)
Submerged speed	8.75kt (16.19km/h)
Range	8,000 miles (12,874km/h) at 10kt (18.5km/h)
Fuel	Diesel 132 tons (134 tonnes)
Submerged endurance	1.5 hours at 8.75kt (16.19km/h), 55 hours at 2.25kt (4.16km/h)
Diving depth	300ft (91.44m)
Armament	11 x 21-in. torpedo tubes (six internal bow, two external bow, two stern-pointing external amidships, one external stern) with 17 torpedoes or 12 mines, 1 x 4-in. gun, 3 x machine guns; *Thrasher* and *Trusty* had 1 x 20mm Oerlikon added in 1943
Complement	61

The bows of this group of submarines were fined in the same manner as *Triumph* and *Thunderbolt*, decreasing the bow wave and improving underwater handling. Also, in order to prevent failure in use, this group had their external bow torpedo doors removed. The loss of streamlining

this caused led to a drop of 0.25kt (0.46km/h) in service, but this was considered acceptable.

The most notable change in design of the 1939 T-Class was the incorporation of a viable stern salvo. Reversing the two amidships torpedo tubes as well as adding an external tube to the stern achieved this. It now meant that the submarine could fire a spread of three torpedoes as it retired, while maintaining the ability to fire eight in one spread from the bow. A minelaying capability was incorporated into all seven boats after successful trials in *Trusty* in 1941. The mines were carried instead of torpedoes and released through the torpedo tubes.

Tempest, *Thorn* and *Thrasher* were fitted with Sulzer engines, *Traveller* and *Trooper* with Admiralty pattern engines and *Trusty* and *Turbulent* with Vickers ones.

1940 War Programme design (Group III)

A further 31 T-Class submarines were completed from the 1940 specification. They were *Taciturn, Tally-Ho, Tantalus, Tantivy, Taurus, Templar, Trespasser, Truculent* and *P311* ordered in 1940; *Taciturn, Talent* (*i*)*, Tapir, Tarn, Tasman* (later *Talent* [*iii*])*, Telemachus, Teredo, Terrapin, Thorough, Thule, Tiptoe, Tireless, Token, Tradewind, Trenchant, Trump* and *Tudor* ordered in 1941; and *Tabard, Thermopylae, Totem, Truncheon* and *Turpin* ordered in 1942.

HMS *Trooper* was lost with all hands in October 1943 in the Aegean. It was probably mined.

SPECIFICATIONS

Length overall	273ft (83.21m)
Maximum width	26ft 7in. (8.1m)
Surface displacement	1,327 tons (1,348 tonnes)
Submerged displacement	1,571 tons (1,596 tonnes)
Bhp engines	2,500 (1,863kW)
Surface speed	15.25kt (28.22km/h)
Bhp motors	1,450 (1,080kW)
Submerged speed	8.75kt (16.19km/h)
Range	11,000 miles (17,702km) at 10kt (18.5km/h)
Fuel	Diesel 230 tons (234 tonnes) max
Submerged endurance	1.5 hours at 8.75kt (16.19km/h), 55 hours at 2.25kt (4.16km/h)
Diving depth	300ft (91.44m) until welded-hull boats, when increased to 350ft (106.68m)
Armament	11 x 21-in. torpedo tubes (six internal bow, two external bow, two external stern-pointing amidships,one external stern) with 17 torpedoes or 12 mines, 1 x 4-in. gun, 3 x machine guns *Thrasher* and *Trusty* had 1 x 20mm Oerlikon cannon added in 1943
Complement	63 (occasionally more)

With the 22 ordered before 1940, a total of 53 T-Class submarines were completed. This is the largest number of a single class of patrol submarine ever operated by the Royal Navy.

During the construction of the boats ordered in 1941, the all-welded hull was introduced. *Taciturn*, *Talent* (*iii*), *Tapir*, *Tarn*, *Teredo*, *Tiptoe* and *Trump* were so completed, as were all of the boats ordered in 1942. This increased diving depth to 350ft (106.68m), although in practice they could go much deeper.

The torpedo arrangement was the same as the 1939 boats, but by now it was realized that external tubes had their problems. Torpedoes could not be serviced and suffered a higher than average failure rate in use. The tubes also affected the streamlining of the boats. They were abandoned in the following A-Class, which was already being designed.

The majority of the T-Class were fitted with the Admiralty-pattern diesel engine, which had been settled upon as the optimum design, a feature also incorporated into the A-Class. As with the S-Class, two freon blowers were fitted to deal with the high temperatures experienced in the Far East. Radar also became standard equipment.

Although late into the war, this last batch of T-Class submarines accounted for six enemy submarines and two cruisers, among many other successes. Many were still new when the war ended and went on to become a major part of the post-war submarine fleet. Some were lengthened in an attempt to increase their range, which had been exposed as their major limiting factor in the Far East during the closing period of the war. The last, *Tiptoe*, was decommissioned in 1969.

THE U-CLASS SUBMARINE

Originally intended as an unarmed submarine to be used to train crews and anti-submarine forces, the U-Class rapidly evolved into a very successful submarine design, belying its small size, low speed and poor range. The U-Class submarine will always be associated with the war in the Mediterranean, the siege of Malta and with the Royal Navy's most successful submarine captain, Lt Cdr M. D. Wanklyn, VC, DSO.

The cramped control room of a U-Class submarine, HMS *Unseen*.

In all, 70 U-Class submarines were completed, although not all of them were to serve in the Royal Navy. The Free French, Dutch, Norwegian, Greek, Danish, Polish and Russian navies were all to operate U-Class submarines at some time.

1936 design (Group I)

The three initial U-Class submarines ordered in 1936 were *Undine*, *Unity* and *Ursula*. They were the only ones ready at the outbreak of the war.

SPECIFICATIONS

Length overall	191ft (58.22m)
Maximum width	16ft 1in. (4.90m)
Surface displacement	630 tons (640 tonnes)
Submerged displacement	730 tons (742 tonnes)
Bhp engines	615 (458kW)
Surface speed	11.25kt (20.82km/h)
Bhp motors	825 (615kW)
Submerged speed	9kt (16.66km/h)
Range	3,800 miles (6,115km) at 10kt (18.5km/h)
Fuel	Diesel 38 tons (39 tonnes)
Submerged endurance	120 miles (193.12km) at 2kt (3.7km/h)
Diving depth	200ft (60.96m)
Armament	6 x 21-in. bow torpedo tubes with ten torpedoes; *Ursula* had six 21-in. bow torpedo tubes with eight torpedoes (or later six mines), 1 x 3-in. gun
Complement	31

Unique among the main three classes of submarine used by the Royal Navy in World War II, the U-Class was of a single hull design, with all fuel and ballast tanks held inside the pressure hull. The hull was of a riveted construction throughout the war, with the U-Class never going over to all-welded hulls, as the S- and T-classes did.

Internally, the submarine was divided by five bulkheads and was equipped with four hatches, two of which were fitted with twill trunks for escape. It was equipped with six ballast tanks and a quick diving or 'Q' tank. Hydraulic power was used to open and close the ballast tanks and to operate the hydroplanes and rudder. As with the S-Class and T-Class, the higher mounted forward hydroplane could be folded against the hull when coming alongside.

The fitting of two external torpedo tubes gave this small submarine a six-torpedo spread – a big punch for its size. However, the external tubes were not a successful innovation. As with the T-Class the external tubes gave the submarine a bulbous appearance at the bow and this caused a large and highly visible bow wave, even at periscope depth (a shallow 12ft/3.66m on U-Class submarines) and also made the submarine difficult to control underwater. On the surface the bow was a hindrance in heavy seas. Even more alarmingly, it was difficult to prevent the submarine from popping to the surface when all six torpedoes were fired in a single spread, owing

The torpedo room of the T-Class HMS *Tribune*. It was not very spacious when carrying a full load.

HMS *Unbroken* struck two cruisers, among other successes. It also turned its gun on several targets, even including bridges.

to the rapid loss of weight. The obvious solution was to remove the external tubes, and this was done on all future boats, with the bow being a more streamlined shape. *Ursula* had its bows reshaped in 1942, but surprisingly it retained its external tubes.

The lack of a deck gun was rectified in *Ursula* with the fitting of a 3-in. gun. Two reload torpedoes had to be sacrificed to compensate for the additional weight. *Ursula* was later fitted to lay mines from its torpedo tubes. *Undine* and *Unity* had already been lost by this time.

A true first in British submarine design was the fitting of the diesel-electric drive system for propulsion. This was a radical departure from the traditional diesel-electric system used in all previous boats. In essence, the diesel-electric drive system utilized the electric motors to turn the propellers at all times. The diesel engines were only used to generate electricity for the motors and to charge the batteries. This system offered benefits over the traditional diesel-electric system because it didn't need a series of complicated clutches and anti-vibration mounts and dampers to alleviate vibration and to couple and decouple the engines.

In wartime service, it became clear that something was wrong with the design of the propellers and outer hull – the propellers cavitated badly and the singing propellers were a danger. In later U-Class submarines, the stern was remodelled, but for the first three vessels the propellers were redesigned and this partially quietened the source of noise.

1939 and subsequent War Emergency design (Group II)
Twelve (nearly half) of the submarines ordered under the War Emergency Programme in 1939 were U-Class submarines. They were *Umpire, Una, Unbeaten, Undaunted, Union, Unique, Upholder, Upright, Urchin, Urge, Usk* and *Utmost*. Nine of these submarines were lost during the war. A further 34 U-Class submarines were completed under the 1940 and 1941 War

HMS *Vampire* at high speed in 1944. It was the first of the new V-Class to patrol from Malta. *Vampire* rammed its first victim, displaying the aggressive approach adopted by many of the later arrivals in the Mediterranean.

Programmes. They were *Ultimatum, Ultor, Umbra, Unbending, Unbroken, Unison, United, Unrivalled, Unruffled, Unruly, Unseen, Unshaken, Uproar, P32, P33, P36, P38, P39, P41, P47, P48* and *P52* in 1940; and *Universal, Unsparing, Unswerving, Untiring, Upstart, Usurper, Uther, Vandal, Varangian, Varne (i), Vitality* (ex-*Untamed*) and *Vox* in 1941.

SPECIFICATIONS

Length overall	191ft (58.22m)
	192ft (58.52m) *Undaunted, Union, Urchin* and *Urge*;
	197ft (60.05m) *Umpire, Una* and (after modification)
	Unbeaten and *Unique* and all 1940–41 boats
Maximum width	16ft (4.88m)
Surface displacement	630 tons (640 tonnes);
	1940–41 boats 658 tons (669 tonnes)
Submerged displacement	732 tons (744 tonnes);
	1940–41 boats 740 tons (752 tonnes)
Bhp engines	615 (458kW)
Surface speed	11.25kt (20.82km/h)
Bhp motors	825 (615kW)
Submerged speed	9kt (16.66km/h)
Range	3,800 miles (6,115kW) at 10kt (18.5km/h);
	5,000 miles (8,047km) at 10kt (18.5km/h) 1940–41 boats
Fuel	Diesel 38 tons (39 tonnes);
	55 tons (56 tonnes) max 1940–41 boats
Submerged endurance	120 miles (193.12km) at 2kt (3.7km/h)
Diving depth	200ft (60.96m)
Armament	4 x 21-in. bow torpedo tubes with eight torpedoes and later six mines, 1 x 12pdr gun, 2 x (later 3 x) machine guns. *Unbeaten* and *Unique* later had their guns upgraded to 3in. All boats ordered in 1940 and 1941 were equipped with the 3-in. gun as standard.
Complement	33 max

Much had been learned from the Group I U-Class and modifications were made to the War Emergency Programme orders. Of note was the omission of the external tubes (although the first few still retained a bulbous bow) and the reshaping of the bows and stern. An unpopular World War I-era 12pdr gun was fitted as standard, although it was later upgraded to a 3-in. gun on *Unbeaten* and *Unique*, and all boats ordered in 1940 and 1941 were completed with the larger gun. Also, the hydroplanes were enlarged to give better underwater handling. The 1940 and 1941 boats were redesigned to carry more fuel and this enhanced their range. Forty-four of these submarines were built by Vickers, most of them at Barrow-in-Furness.

The accidental loss of *Vandal* and *Untamed* whilst undergoing training led to an inquiry into the likelihood of sabotage carried out by the Secret Service. The inquiry report is still classified.

In July 1940, the Admiralty ceased to give new submarines individual names, but elected to number them only (as had been the tradition into the 1920s), and hence six U-Class, one S-Class and one T-Class were sunk without receiving a name. The policy was reversed in 1942 at the command of

In February 1945 HMS *Venturer* became the first submarine in history to sink another submerged submarine. The salvo was fired on an Asdic bearing at *U864*, which was travelling using a *Schnorchel* (snorkel), allowing it to remain submerged throughout its patrol.

Winston Churchill. This gave the Admiralty a problem naming so many boats beginning with the letter U. It is therefore understandable that some of the later U-Class submarines had some rather unique names. It is unlikely that the Royal Navy will reuse such names as *Uproar*, *Unruffled* and *Unsparing* in the future. Even when, by force of necessity, words beginning with V were used, some idiosyncratic names emerged.

V-Class (Group III)

The final specification of the U-Class appeared in the War Emergency Programmes of 1941–42. A further 21 submarines were completed to this design. They were *Upshot*, *Urtica*, *Vagabond*, *Varience*, *Venturer*, *Vigorous*, *Viking*, *Vampire*, *Varne* (*ii*), *Veldt*, *Vineyard*, *Virtue*, *Visigoth*, *Vivid*, *Voracious*, *Votary*, *Vox* (*ii*), *Virulent*, *Volatile*, *Vortex* and *Vulpine*.

SPECIFICATIONS	
Length overall	205ft (62.48ft)
Maximum width	16ft (4.88m)
Surface displacement	662 tons (673 tonnes)
Submerged displacement	740 tons (752 tonnes)
Bhp engines	800 (596kW)
Surface speed	12.75kt (23.59km/h)
Bhp motors	760 (566kW)
Submerged speed	9kt (16.66km/h)
Range	5,000 miles (8,047km) at 10kt (18.5km/h)
Fuel	55 tons (56 tonnes) max
Submerged endurance	120 miles (193.12km) at 2kt (3.7km/h)
Diving depth	300ft (91.44m)
Armament	4 x 21-in. bow torpedo tubes with eight torpedoes and later six mines, 1 x 12pdr gun, 3 x machine guns
Complement	37 max

These submarines represent the final refinement of the U-Class concept. Hulls were lengthened further to reduce the still-present propeller noise and further to streamline the bows. The hull frames were now of a welded design, enabling a thicker steel to be used on the still-riveted pressure hull. An increase in diving depth to 300ft (91.44m) resulted. Again, all of these vessels were built by Vickers.

No V-boats were lost during the war, and not all saw action. However, *Venturer* became the first submarine in history to sink another submarine while both were underwater. It also achieved the rare distinction of sinking two U-boats.

OTHER BRITISH SUBMARINE CLASSES

A variety of earlier submarine classes was available for action in 1939. They ranged from smaller patrol submarines to minelayers and overseas designs. While some served with greater success than others, a combination of age and obsolescence, coupled with their early deployment in the darkest days of the war, meant that over half those deployed were sunk in action. As the war progressed, Lend Lease and captured submarines briefly served with the Royal Navy. Some of these too were lost in action.

H-Class

Nine of these World War I relics remained in service in 1939. They were used operationally in 1940–41, despite numerous defects. A trusty and popular submarine design when built, the H-boats were somewhat aged by 1939. *H28* had the distinction of being the only submarine to have made war patrols in both world wars. Two were lost before the remainder were withdrawn for training roles.

L-Class

Three of these late World War I patrol submarines were still in service in 1939. They were used in operations in 1940 before being turned over for training. They were later sent to Canada for the same purpose. None were lost in action.

Porpoise

Ordered in 1930, *Porpoise* was the first minelayer built specifically for this task for the Royal Navy. It carried 50 mines externally on its casing and could carry more internally as a replacement for the usual 12 torpedoes. It also carried a powerful 4.7-in. gun.

Porpoise's design proved to be highly successful, making minelaying a safer and simpler task than previously. Displacing over 2,000 tons (2,032 tonnes) when submerged, it was large and potentially cumbersome. However, *Porpoise* was popular with its experienced crew and it led a charmed life in service in the Mediterranean and Far East, laying 465 mines and sinking several ships, until, in 1945, it became the last Royal Navy submarine sunk in action.

Grampus-Class

A further five minelaying submarines of improved Porpoise design were built just before hostilities began: *Cachalot*, *Grampus*, *Narwhal*, *Rorqual* and *Seal*. They were a good and comfortable design and were widely used during the war. Two were lost on their maiden patrols and only *Rorqual* was to survive.

The minelayer HMS *Rorqual* was the only one of the six pre-war minelayers of its class to survive the war. Note the open stern door to the mine compartment in the upper casing.

The capture of *Seal* by the Germans in 1940 was a propaganda coup for them. Renamed *UB*, the submarine was used for training and evaluation by the Kriegsmarine before being scrapped. *Seal's* commander suffered the ordeal of a court martial on his return from captivity, but he was exonerated of all blame for the loss.

O-, P- and R-classes

These nearly indistinguishable classes of overseas patrol submarine were the first such designs to emerge after World War I. The submarines were constructed with long patrols in the Far East in mind and were similar in displacement to the minelayers built during the same time. The submarines were well armed with eight torpedo tubes and a 4.7-in. gun each, and all with a decent endurance. However, in use numerous problems emerged with their overall design. All suffered from leaks at diving depth. Reliability problems continually emerged, not least with the engines, which were a constant source of trouble. Several suffered from leaking fuel tanks, which needed expensive refitting with welded replacements. Nonetheless, a total of 18 were ready for service in 1939. No fewer than 12 of these somewhat unlucky submarines would be sunk during the war before the remainder were removed from frontline service in 1942–43.

River-Class

The River-Class represented the only close-to-successful design of fleet submarine employed by the Royal Navy. These submarines, built to operate with the fleet under diesel power, managed to reach the unprecedented speed of 22kt (40.71km/h) on the surface. Sadly, this coincided with a considerable increase in speed of the battlefleet, with several units achieving speeds in excess of 30kt (55.52km/h). Nevertheless, their high speed was to prove an asset in wartime.

These submarines were well armed, with six internal bow torpedoes and a 4-in. or 4.7-in. gun. Their high speed and large cargo-carrying capacity made them excellent supply submarines, a role which *Severn* and *Clyde* played in the Mediterranean. Of the pre-war designs, the River-Class submarines could justifiably have claimed to be the most successful in service, with only *Thames* being sunk during the war. *Clyde* put a torpedo into the German battlecruiser *Gneisenau* in 1940 and later had a fight with three U-boats at the same time. *Severn* later claimed the Italian submarine *Bianchi*.

The large pre-war HMS *Oxley* became the first British submarine to be sunk in the war. Tragically, it was sunk in error by HMS *Triton*.

OPERATIONS, 1939–40

The 'phoney' war

The opening months of the war saw British submarines and their German counterparts take on much the same roles as in 1918. British submarines were deployed against predominantly naval targets.

It was envisioned that the submarine's primary role would be in forming reconnaissance units for the Home Fleet, reporting on any unusual activity by major German surface units. Submarines were therefore sent to operate off Heligoland and to sweep to the south-west of Norway. This was an important role, because the Coastal Command Anson aircraft did not possess enough range to patrol off the coast of Norway at this time.

Of primary concern was the possibility of 'blue on blue' incidents between friendly forces. This remained a problem in home waters throughout the war, and was sadly highlighted on 10 September 1939 when *Triton*, in its billet, albeit out of position, encountered a surfaced submarine and made a challenge by Aldis lamp. The reply received was unsatisfactory and *Triton* fired a spread of three torpedoes at the now supposed U-boat, one of which hit and sank *Oxley*. Coming straight from reserve, it is unlikely that *Oxley* was properly worked up at the time of this incident.

Attacks by the aircraft of Coastal Command were also a major concern, with several reported in the opening months of the war. *Seahorse* was attacked twice; *Sterlet* and *Seawolf* also reported unwanted incidents with the RAF. Despite the designation of submarine exercise areas, bombing-free areas around transiting submarines and the escorting of outward-bound and returning submarines, incidents still occurred. They were primarily due to poor navigation by both sides and a reluctance on the part of submarines to use recognition flares, in case they attracted enemy aircraft.

Luck began to swing the way of the British in November when *Sturgeon* became the first British submarine of the war to sink an enemy ship. On 20 September, off the declared German minefield to the west of Denmark, it successfully torpedoed the anti-submarine ship *V209*.

Two weeks later, north of the German-declared minefield, *Salmon* finally sank a U-boat. *U36* became the first of 39 enemy submarines sunk or damaged by British submarines during the war. December also witnessed *Triumph*'s near miraculous escape when it struck a mine north of the German-declared area. The bows were completely blown off, but the internal torpedo doors held. Legend has it that a rating slept in the fore ends throughout the entire incident.

In January 1940, the legendary Vice Adm Max Horton, KCB, DSO* (the asterisk indicates that a bar was conferred), took command of British submarine operations. His arrival coincided with the first three war losses to the Germans. *Seahorse* was mined in the Bight of Heligoland, and became the first British submarine lost to the enemy during the war. Shortly thereafter, German anti-submarine ships in the same area sank *Undine* and *Starfish*, taking their entire crews prisoner. This came as a shock, because the German vessels were known not to have Asdic. The submarines were sunk in shallow water, where the German hydrophones were good enough to detect their targets. Both submarines had initially given away their positions by making attacks. As a result, Horton ordered

Lt Cdr E. O. Bickford, DSO, at the periscope of HMS *Salmon*. His damaging of two German cruisers and the sinking of a U-boat in December 1939 were considerable morale-boosters and won him early promotion.

British submarine patrols farther offshore into deeper waters, where the German hydrophones were expected not to be so effective.

Throughout the 'phoney' war period, British submarines had cut their teeth in difficult circumstances and while they had not achieved great things, they had proved that they could operate off hostile shores and under the constant threat of aircraft and anti-submarine shipping. Four submarines had been lost, but two cruisers had been damaged and a U-boat sunk. More submarines were coming online, with a net increase of six frontline boats available at the beginning of April 1940. In that month, Germany embarked on the invasion of Norway.

The Norway campaign

Horton foresaw the invasion of Norway, albeit for the wrong reasons. He had planned to force the merchant shipping out into the open sea by laying minefields by submarine in coastal waters, using neutral Norway, Sweden and Denmark. He hoped this would enable Allied submarines to interrupt the iron ore trade to Germany, still by prize rules. This action, he concluded, would probably force Germany to close the Skagerrak by seizing Norway. So, on 4 April, *Narwhal* laid the first submarine-laid minefield of the war across the ore trade route, while the submarine presence in the Skagerrak was increased.

On 8 April, most of the German invasion fleet slipped past the British submarine *Unity*, on patrol off Horns Reef in the dark. It was detected by Coastal Command, but by the time the Home Fleet was readied, German troops were on Norwegian soil. In the Kattegat, *Trident* and the Polish *Orzel* did sink two supply ships by the prize rules, although *Triton* missed a naval invasion force, led by *Blücher*, at long range.

A day later, *Thistle* was sunk by a U-boat off Stavanger. However, it was the British submarines that were to have the more successful day. *Truant* was off Kristiansand when it spotted *Karlsruhe* returning from the invasion. Wisely, a spread of all ten torpedoes was fired at medium range. Two hit and sank the cruiser. *Sunfish* added to this tally with a 7,000-ton (7,112-tonne) freighter off the Skaw.

Now alerted to the invasion, the British War Cabinet finally authorized unrestricted submarine warfare in the Skagerrak. Allied submarines could now be used to full effect. *Sunfish* added another vessel to the tally that evening. Sadly, on the same day *Tarpon* was counter-attacked and sunk by an escort west of northern Denmark.

Disappointingly, and despite a great effort using 17 Allied submarines to intercept them, *Scharnhorst*, *Gneisenau* and *Hipper* all managed to reach Wilhelmshaven undetected on the 12th. The reasons these large ships

The pre-war minelayer HMS *Seal* became the only British submarine to fall into German hands, when it was mined off Denmark in May 1940. The survivors were interned until 1945, when the captain and surviving officer suffered the added indignity of a court martial. They were acquitted.

were not detected were poor surface visibility, coupled with excellent radio direction finding by shore-based elements of the Axis, which were able to pick up the radio transmissions from the submarines and pinpoint their positions, then relay this information to the German ships. This process had already thwarted previous Allied attempts to intercept valuable German surface elements.

On 29 April, *Unity*, outward bound on patrol, was run over and sunk by a Norwegian freighter shortly after leaving Blyth; four were killed. A few days later Allied troops began to withdraw from central Norway, signalling the beginning of the end of the Norwegian campaign.

Countering the invasion of Norway cost Britain five submarines: *Thistle*, *Tarpon*, *Sterlet*, *Seal* and *Unity*. Due to Horton's foresight though, the submarines had been well placed to report the passing of the invasion force in the Kattegat. Two large warships were successfully attacked in the Skagerrak and a moderately successful campaign against supply shipping had been conducted. However, the Royal Navy had failed to prevent the invasion.

In reality, submarines were all that Britain had to counter the invasion, because the Home Fleet had effectively lost control of the Skagerrak and south Norway to the Luftwaffe. The limited number of submarines available and the speed of the invasion, coupled with the summer daylight hours, ensured that only a little of the materiel and only two battalions of troops shipped to invade Norway were sunk by submarine. This tally was still far more than any other British arm could claim. If anything, British submarines proved they could operate under Axis air cover, where the fleet could not. Such capability was to increase their perceived importance as the war went on.

On 10 May, Germany attacked the Low Countries and the focus of the war moved away from Norway. Nevertheless, submarine operations continued in the North Sea and Skagerrak until August. It proved to be a very difficult time for British submarines. Close patrols along the Norwegian coast in summer were near impossible because of the constant daylight. Nevertheless, *Clyde* spotted the battlecruiser *Gneisenau* and at a range of 4,000 yards (3,656m) fired six torpedoes at it. One scored a hit, which forced *Gneisenau* back into port.

As the Germans now reverted to attacking merchant shipping in the Atlantic, encounters with U-boats began to increase as they were seen transiting through the North Sea. No attacks made at this time were successful. This was fortunate for *Clyde*, which missed a submarine with a spread of six torpedoes – the target later turned out to be *Truant*. The U-boats were more successful and the tables turned on 1 August, when *Spearfish* was torpedoed by *U34* while passing across the North Sea. There was only one survivor.

The highest concentration of British submarines in home waters was during the fight for Norway. From then on submarines stationed in home waters reverted to the roles of 1939 and operated mainly in support of the Admiralty's home waters strategy as the war evolved.

Vice Adm Sir Max Horton, KCB, DSO*, commanded the submarine force for three years and oversaw the resurgence of the service. He went on to defeat the U-boats as Admiral Western Approaches. This most brilliant of leaders was also a submariner of repute, being the first British commander to sink a German naval vessel in World War I.

An early S-Class, HMS *Sturgeon*, struck the first blow against the Kriegsmarine when it destroyed an escort in November 1939.

THE MEDITERRANEAN

At the outbreak of the war, the British Navy was twice as large as the Italian Navy, although it had many other commitments. The British and French navies had local superiority in the western and eastern Mediterranean, but not in the central area. This situation explains why Britain opted to send its supply traffic around the Cape instead of through the Suez Canal. The central Mediterranean was controlled by the Italian Air Force, supported by its fleet and its submarines. The Italian strategy was focused on maintaining this position. It gained little from seeking action because it could not make good its losses, while Britain, in theory at least, could send in more forces from home waters or from the Far East. For the British, this strategic situation was suited to submarines, which could operate in seas controlled by enemy air elements. British submarines were to play a crucial role in cutting supplies to Africa and forcing the Axis onto the back foot. The price paid was high.

In 1940, strained British relations with Italy led to the transfer of ten submarines from the Far East and Indian Ocean to Alexandria, along with the depot ship *Medway* from Singapore. The First Submarine Flotilla was established and its 12 submarines were *Parthian*, *Phoenix*, *Proteus*, *Pandora*, *Grampus*, *Rorqual*, *Odin*, *Orpheus*, *Olympus*, *Otus* and the two already in the Mediterranean, *Otway* and *Osiris*. Six, including the two minelayers *Grampus* and *Rorqual*, were based at Malta.

War with Italy

Ten days after war broke out with Italy on 10 June 1940, 45 out of 46 of the French submarines in the eastern Mediterranean surrendered and Britain stood virtually alone. Interestingly, *Pandora* and *Proteus* were ordered to watch the French fleets at Algiers and Oran respectively. Confusion at command level over what these submarines were actually to do if they sighted French units led to *Pandora* sinking the French sloop *Rigault de Genouille*. The subsequent apologies sent by Britain to France ring hollow when the subsequent destruction of the French battlefleet in Oran four days later is considered.

The first patrols out from Alexandria were made to cover the major Italian fleet bases. *Phoenix* and *Rorqual* were ordered to screen a supply convoy heading for Alexandria from Malta. *Phoenix* sighted the Italian battlefleet and successfully made a contact report that led to the indecisive battle of Calabria. *Phoenix* did not survive this patrol, being sunk on 16 July by an Italian torpedo boat after missing it with a torpedo attack.

On 18 July unrestricted submarine warfare was permitted within 30 miles (48km) of the Italian coastline, thus allowing attacks upon the Libyan supply route. On 31 July *Oswald* was sunk by Italian destroyers off Messina. It had made a contact report the previous day and had been located by radio direction finding. A sweep at night by five Italian destroyers located the submarine on the surface. All but three of its crew were rescued and taken into captivity. The locating of this submarine by direction finding bears similarity to the Norwegian campaign and would lead in due course to a much more judicious use of the radio by submarines on patrol.

The depot ship *Medway* sinks after being torpedoed by a submarine, *U372*, while being transferred to Haifa from Alexandria in June 1942. The loss of this vital source of replenishment dealt a tough blow to the British submarine force in the Mediterranean at a crucial time.

The loss of *Oswald* was the low water mark for the British submarine force in the Mediterranean theatre. Five submarines had been sunk and with two under repair in Malta, the number of available boats fell to just five, although reinforcements from the Far East and home waters were being organized. Against this, the only vessels that had been sunk were an Italian submarine, a French sloop and a troopship (which fell victim to a mine laid by *Rorqual*).

During the next five months to the end of 1940, Britain lost another four submarines, a bleak time for the British submarine force. Although the lifting of the prize rules led to a rise in successes, it only equated to nine ships sunk in the next five months. This represented less than 1 per cent of shipping being sent to reinforce the Italian forces in Libya. By comparison, Britain lost nine submarines in the same period, representing half of the available force. The first five had fallen victim to Italian surface forces, but after this the Axis minefields began to take a steady toll of Allied submarines.

The Italian Navy, like their German counterparts in the North Sea, did not have Asdic, but possessed only hydrophones. Their success in sinking five submarines is in no small measure due to the size of the British submarines and the lack of realistic war training in the Far East bases, from where they had been transferred. Undoubtedly, accurate pinpointing of submarine locations by radio direction finding had made up for the absence of Asdic.

The performance of British submarines against Italy in 1940 can only be considered to have been largely unsuccessful. Disappointingly, the chances to attack heavy Italian warships had not been taken. Losses were high and successes few. Supply channels to Greece and Africa were largely untouched. In mitigation, it should be pointed out that no other arm achieved even this level of sinkings at the time.

The first few months of 1941 saw fortunes begin to change for the British. Ten new U-Class submarines arrived and were based at Malta. This coincided with the arrival of Cdr G. W. G. 'Shrimp' Simpson to take command of submarine operations from the island. The larger submarines still surviving were sent to operate from Alexandria and they received a minelayer and three T-boats as reinforcements. The Malta-based U-Class submarines were used primarily to patrol the Tunisian coast. Patrols also covered the Messina Straits and Ionian Sea. In February, the newly arrived *Upright* made its presence felt by carrying out a night surface attack on the Italian cruiser *Armando Diaz*, which sank after being struck by one torpedo. This was the most spectacular success so far achieved by the British submarine force in the Mediterranean. In the

A: The evolution of the T-Class submarine

1

2

3

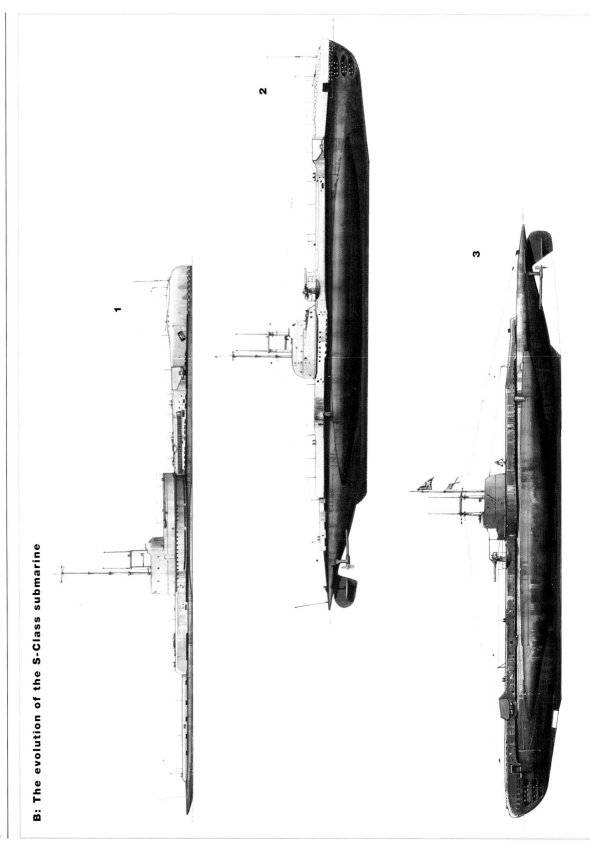

B: The evolution of the S-Class submarine

B

C: The evolution of the U-Class submarine

1

2

3

D: GROUP III DESIGN, T-CLASS SUBMARINE OF 1944

KEY

1 Rudder
2 Auxiliary tank
3 After hydroplane
4 Stabilizing fin and hydroplane guard
5 Steering gear
6 Torpedo tube
7 Torpedo davit
8 Stokers' mess
9 5th watertight bulkhead
10 Engine exhaust trunk
11 MF DF coil
12 Jumping wire
13 Torpedo tubes
14 Asdic type 138 B
15 4th watertight bulkhead

16 Watertight office
17 Radar office
18 Conning tower
19 20mm Oerlikon
20 Look out platforms
21 Type 268W SW RDF
22 7.5-in. low power periscope
23 9.5-in. high power periscope
24 Type 291W AW RDF
25 Voice pipe to bridge
26 Main WT aerial
27 4-in. Mk XII gun
28 Ward room
29 Passage
30 Main tank

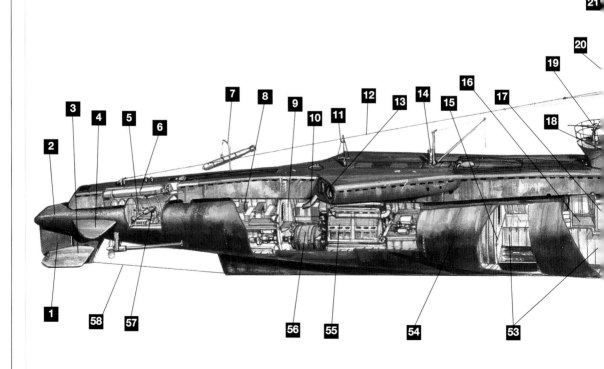

31 Jumping wire
32 Torpedo derrick
33 Seamen's mess
34 W.C.
35 2nd watertight bulkhead
36 Torpedo loading hatch
37 Torpedo stowage compartment (6 torpedoes)
38 1st watertight bulkhead
39 Fore hydroplane (turned in)
40 Torpedo tubes
41 Obstruction rod
42 Asdic type 129
43 Oil fuel tanks
44 Bilge pump

45 Fresh water tank
46 Batteries
47 Bunks and lockers
48 Cold cupboard
49 Magazine
50 3rd watertight bulkhead
51 Commanding officer's cabin
52 Batteries
53 Oil fuel tanks
54 Main tank no. 6
55 Main engines
56 Main motors
57 Hydroplane gear
58 Obstruction wire

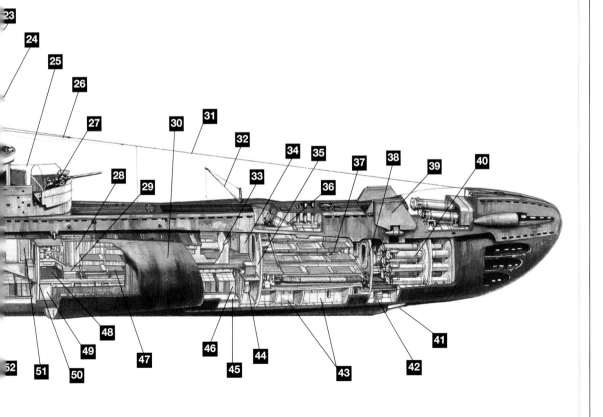

**E: Other submarine designs that fought
in World War II**

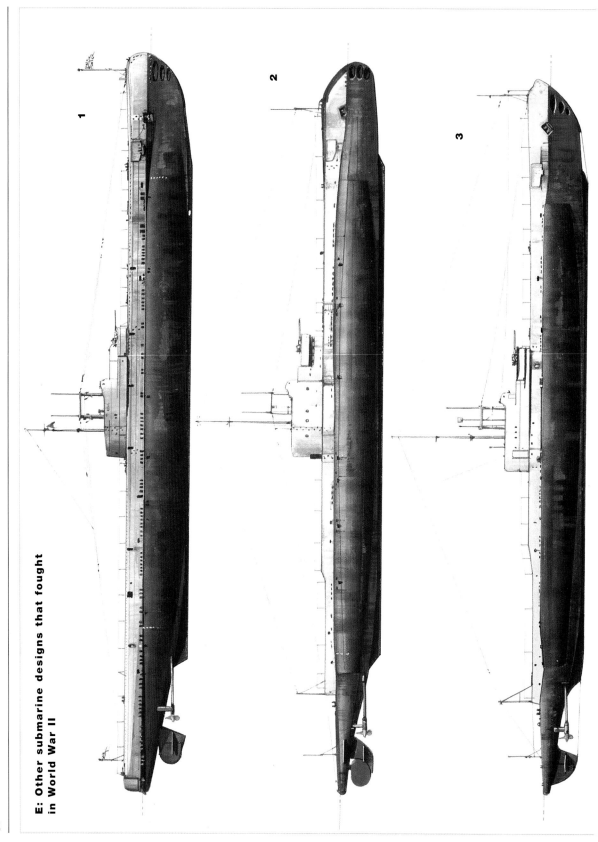

1

2

3

F: *Safari* attacks coastal shipping

F

G: U-Class returns to Malta

G

The hole in HMS *Thrasher*'s conning tower was caused by a bomb that failed to detonate (another was found in the casing). Their removal by Lt P. W. S. Roberts and PO T. W. Gould won the pair Victoria Crosses.

same month, the British government expanded the sink-on-sight zone so that it became possible to operate against the entire Libyan supply route.

Another notable success came at the end of March when the ever-reliable *Rorqual* sank the Italian submarine *Capponi*, with a double hit from five torpedoes fired. In the previous five days, it had additionally sunk two freighters and successfully laid a minefield in which another ship had been destroyed. *P31* also carried out an attack during the month, which is remarkable because the sea was so calm that the periscope could not be used safely. Therefore, using Asdic alone, *P31* closed its target to 800 yards (731m) and hit with all four torpedoes, sinking the 5,000-ton (5,080 tonne) freighter. This is an almost unique event and won Lt J. B. de B. Kershaw the DSO.

On 25 April *Upholder*, under the command of Lt Cdr Wanklyn, sank a 5,400-ton (5,486-tonne) freighter off Tunisia. Two more were sunk on 1 May, adding 9,300 tons (9,449 tonnes) to *Upholder*'s tonnage tally. This was the beginning of a successful run of sinkings by what became Britain's most successful submarine of the war.

To summarize, in the first six months of 1941, only two British submarines were lost, both to mines. By contrast, the Italians lost around 130,000 tons (132,080 tonnes) of shipping. The rate of sinking on the African supply route was low, however, with fewer than two ships a month being sunk – the Afrika Korps was successfully transported to Africa during this time. Less than 5 per cent of this shipping was sunk by submarine.

Germany's attack on the Soviet Union in June 1941 changed the strategic balance in the central zone. With the Luftwaffe largely gone, the Allies were able to build up their air strength in Malta and to bring surface forces into the central Mediterranean. Nevertheless, Rommel recaptured Cyrenaica and the supply route between Italy and Benghazi opened. This route received the attention of British submarines, as did Tripoli, the Tyrrhenian Sea and the Aegean. Patrols were backed up by much-improved intelligence due to the reading of the Italian naval cipher and the decryption of Enigma signals being achieved in as little as a few days. Caution was taken not to give away the true extent of the intelligence breakthrough and aircraft were always stationed over enemy convoys before the submarines arrived. In this way, it made each interception look as if air reconnaissance had detected the convoys.

A notable intelligence-led success involved the sinking of the 11,400-ton (11,582-tonne) troopship *Esperia*, by *Unique* off Tripoli in August. The size and course of the convoy, being mustered for a run to Tripoli, was discovered by intelligence work and several submarines were diverted to intercept it. The convoy was well protected by aircraft and escorts and it was with considerable skill that *Unique* was able to acquire a firing position. Two escorts actually passed right over the submarine during the attack.

The battles of Malta and the convoys

On 1 September 1941, the Malta submarines were organized into their own command, named the Tenth Flotilla, under the newly promoted Capt Simpson. The Tenth Flotilla was to become the most famous in the history of British submarines. It is sobering to consider that it suffered the highest rate of losses.

The successes of the legendary 'Fighting Tenth' were in no small part down to the excellent work of the intelligence arm, which again discovered the sailing time, composition and route of another important convoy in September. After confirmation of the departure had been received by air, Simpson stationed *Upholder*, *Upright*, *Unbeaten* and *Ursula* across the likely track of the convoy. It contained three large troopships, *Oceania*, *Neptunia* and *Vulcania*, packed with soldiers, and was escorted by six destroyers. *Unbeaten* found the convoy and made a contact report, before following the convoy in an attempt to close range. *Upholder* was better situated and with a torpedo each from a full spread of four, hit the overlapping *Oceania* and *Neptunia*, the latter ship sinking at once while the other stopped. *Upholder* reloaded and finished off *Oceania* just before *Unbeaten* arrived to do the same job. *Vulcania* was missed by *Ursula* at long range.

The Royal Navy's most successful submarine commander, M. D. Wanklyn, VC, DSO (centre), with some of the crew of HMS *Upholder*. Wanklyn's death at the height of the Mediterranean submarine campaign was a heavy blow to the service.

The sinking of four troopships by British submarines in a few weeks represented a disaster for the Italians. British submarines had their successes against naval targets as well. Importantly, in December the new battleship *Vittoria Veneto* was damaged by *Urge*. The attack was carried out at the range of 3,000 yards (3,048m) by four torpedoes, one of which hit under the forward turret, putting this new and most dangerous ship out of action for over three months.

In the second six months of 1941, Britain lost six submarines. Four were mined and two sunk by anti-submarine ships after revealing their positions by making attacks. However, during this time 13 new submarines had arrived in the Mediterranean, bringing the overall net strength to 28. The second half of 1941 had been successful for the British submarine force. It had more than compensated for its slow start and had clearly demonstrated that it was an efficient means of cutting off supplies to the Axis in Africa. The Mediterranean was to continue to utilize the majority of the new submarines available to the British.

For the Axis army in North Africa to perform at its optimal level, it needed around 50,000 tons (50,800 tonnes) of supplies per month. By the middle of 1941, the Allies had seriously compromised its supply chain. The Germans began to react to the loss of supplies to Africa in late 1941. In September, the first of the U-boats arrived in the Mediterranean. Their impact was immediate and decisive. In November *Ark Royal*, the only Allied aircraft carrier in the Mediterranean, was sunk. The Axis fight-back in the Mediterranean reached its peak in 1942 and it became the pivotal year of the war in this theatre. Italian anti-submarine forces began receiving German sonar sets in February and started a rapid construction programme of anti-submarine corvettes. German E-boats were shipped overland for operations in the Mediterranean. The E-boats appeared in February and rapidly laid over 500 mines around the island. The effect of this, combined with Luftwaffe heavy bombing on the Allies' only base of operations in the central Mediterranean, was catastrophic. By March the air force based in Malta had been crushed, three submarines had been damaged and the cruisers and destroyers had been withdrawn.

HMS *Upholder* (left) and *Urge* (right) in Malta. Note the finer bow of *Urge*, a modification in later construction based on wartime experience. Both of these submarines were lost.

However, the British submarines put up a brave fight at sea. On 5 January 1942 *Upholder* was in action again. On this occasion, with its last torpedo it claimed the Italian submarine *St. Bon*. Remarkably this shot was fired by eye only at the onrushing submarine as it opened fire with its deck gun. Axis submarine killing continued on the 12th when *Unbeaten* sank *U374* south-east of Messina with two hits from a full spread of four torpedoes. These successes, plus six other vessels sunk and damaged, were tempered by the loss of *Triumph* to a mine off Athens some time after the 9th. It will be remembered that on 23 December 1939 it had struck a mine in the North Sea and miraculously (for a submarine) survived and returned to base.

In February, *Upholder* was responsible for two of the six supply ships sunk that month. Alarmingly, however, the German-manufactured Asdic sets began to make their appearance at sea. They were responsible for the destruction of two British submarines. The Asdic-equipped Italian torpedo boat *Circe* had been involved in both these sinkings, boding badly for Allied submarines in the future.

In March, British submarines achieved more notable successes. Of note was *Torbay*'s penetration of the anchorage at Corfu, where for 20 hours it hunted for targets and sank a 5,000-ton (5,080-tonne) freighter. In the same month, *Upholder* was successful again, sinking its second submarine in three months when *Tricheco* was hit off Brindisi by two out of four torpedoes fired.

A major success was achieved by *Urge* at the beginning of April, when it hit the cruiser *Bande Nere* with two torpedoes from long range, causing it to sink. However, this success was tempered by the loss of *Upholder* on its 25th patrol. It was detected submerged by a flying boat covering a convoy off Tripoli and depth charged by the escort *Pegaso*. This was a foul blow to the Tenth Flotilla and the Royal Navy in general, coming at a most difficult time.

It was the E-boat-laid minefields and the gradual erosion of the island's air defences that proved to be the deciding factors. With all of the minesweepers sunk, the island had to be abandoned as a base of operations in April, with two submarines mined as they withdrew. *Urge* was sunk on 27 April. It had just been responsible for the sinking of a cruiser and had been a successful boat. *Olympus* was sunk on 8 May. *Una* was the last to leave.

Overall submarine strength fell in April to only 12 boats, even though 11 new U-Class submarines arrived from home waters. Older boats had to be refitted in Britain and three submarines of the Dutch force based at Gibraltar were sent to the Far East. Nevertheless British submarines still managed to sink 117,000 tons (118,872 tonnes) of shipping, the *Bande Nere*, a destroyer and six submarines. The true picture, though, was that the depleted submarine force only managed to prevent around 6 per cent of the Africa Korps' supplies from reaching them. This was much higher than the achievements of air or surface forces, for which the loss of Malta was more serious. Larger submarines were still being used to convey desperately needed supplies to Malta.

With the Mediterranean battlefleet out of action, the supply convoys to Malta needed advance notice of any incursion by the Italian main fleet, so submarines were posted outside the Italian Navy's main anchorages. In March, this strategy worked when *P36* warned that the Italian battlefleet had set out from Taranto and gave the first indication of its movements before the battle of Sirte.

In June, a British convoy attempted to force its way to Malta from Gibraltar. Nine British submarines (nearly all those available) screened its north flank. Disappointingly, when the Italian battlefleet was sighted by *P35*, its attack missed, primarily because the line of ships veered off course sharply due to air attack at the crucial moment. Later, *P35* had success, finishing off the damaged cruiser *Trento*, but the convoy had no option but to turn away and steam back to Gibraltar. U-boats also remained a menace at this time, sinking two British cruisers, *Naiad* and *Hermione*. From July, their attentions were focused on disrupting the Malta supply line.

Believing Malta had been destroyed as a base of operations, and deciding against invasion, the Luftwaffe returned to Russia in May, having pulverized the island for five months. This proved a decisive moment. Malta was far from finished and by July, with aircraft flying off aircraft carriers, its air force had become strong enough to beat off an attack by the remaining Axis aircraft. The victory gave the Allies the confidence they needed to re-establish submarine operations from the island.

With new submarines coming online and others returning from refit, Allied submarine strength had passed its low point of the year and by July had reached 23 operational submarines. The numbers increased further later in the year and the Gibraltar Flotilla was soon operating its own submarines. The eastern base was re-established in the old French submarine base at Beirut. So, in as little as three months after the Tenth Flotilla had been forced from its home in Malta, British submarines were again resurgent. Allied torpedo bombers were also arriving in increasing numbers and began to deplete the Axis supply convoys to Africa.

In August, a major convoy movement to Malta, Operation *Pedestal*, was launched. Eight British submarines protected this very important convoy. *P42* managed to attack and damage the cruisers *Bolzano* and *Attendolo*, putting them permanently out of the war. They were, in fact, retiring for lack of air support. With the Italian battlefleet moored up due to lack of fuel, the attack on Operation *Pedestal* was carried out by Axis submarines, which took a heavy toll of the convoy, sinking or damaging several freighters, a tanker and three cruisers, and destroying the aircraft carrier *Eagle*. While *Pedestal* took up much of the available submarine force, some were able to support the air attacks on the North Africa convoys and in August successes rose sharply with British submarines sinking eight ships, compared to one in July. By September, the submarines were back in force on the convoy lanes and their share of sinkings (another six ships) outstripped those of the RAF.

Operation *Torch* to Operation *Husky*

British submarines began preparing for Operation *Torch*, the American landings in North Africa, in October 1942, yet still they sank 12 ships and a destroyer. In the months from July, however, they had suffered only two losses.

Lt Cdr A. C. C. Miers, VC. In command of HMS *Torbay*, he spent 20 hours in Corfu harbour (including a recharge) and claimed two ships. For this feat and his overall aggressive performance he won the Victoria Cross. In recent years he has become a controversial figure for allegedly mistreating survivors of sunken ships.

Lt A. C. G. Mars (left) in HMS *Unbroken*'s control room in 1943. His attack on the Italian cruisers *Attendolo* and *Bolzano*, in which both were damaged, is noteworthy. Mars became a prolific writer after the war.

Montgomery retook Cyrenaica in November, while the Americans made their *Torch* landings in Morocco on 8 November, which were covered by the British submarines from the Mediterranean and home waters. The submarines were also used to cover the French base of Toulon, and screen the channels around Messina, Sardinia and Sicily. Submarines also acted as navigational beacons, because they could arrive stealthily and get an accurate positional fix in advance of the landings. British submarines carried out this task along the North African coast, while US submarines covered the Atlantic side.

The Axis occupied Tunisia as a countermeasure to *Torch* and landed troops there by air. December saw a huge push by the Italians to supply the Axis in Tunisia. They managed to land 60,000 tons (60,960 tonnes) of supplies, despite losing 16 ships to submarines and more to air attack. Four British submarines were lost in November and December.

The first half of 1943 marked the finale of the war against the Axis shipping lanes to North Africa. The occupation of Tunisia had obliged Italy to continue to maintain a lifeline to the Axis, even though it was becoming increasingly difficult to do so. The Allied air forces gained almost total control over the central zone from bases in Malta and Africa and, therefore, were well situated to decimate the Italian supply effort. Moreover, Allied submarine strength had grown to 32 and the Gibraltar Flotilla moved to Algiers. Patrolling was conducted off the eastern coast of Tunisia and off Sicily. The submarine minelayers laid mines outside Tunis.

While Allied aircraft sank the higher share of ships, submarines contributed 33 vessels sunk in the convoys. After mid-April, only one large ship reached Tunisia and the Axis in North Africa finally surrendered the following month.

British submarine operations were not only aimed at the Italy–Tunisia convoys. They patrolled wherever targets could be found. During the first five months of 1943, submarines destroyed more ships at sea than any other force, but Allied aircraft devastated ships at anchor and in total achieved around 50 per cent of the ships sunk in this period. By comparison submarines accounted for 29 per cent. However, this was the hiatus of submarine success so far, during which over 47 merchant vessels and many smaller craft of various sizes were sunk. A number of naval targets were also destroyed, the most important of which were *P44*'s (*United*) sinking of the destroyer *Bombardieri* off Marittimo in January and the sinking of *U301* off western Corsica by *P212* in the same month. *P44* had been kept down for 36 hours after its attack, the longest submergence by a British submarine during the war. The crew were sick upon breathing fresh air on surfacing.

The price for the submarine arm's success was the loss of seven submarines. Of particular note was the loss of *Turbulent*. Its commander, formerly of *Pandora*, Cdr J. W. 'Tubby' Linton, DSO, DSC, was one of the outstanding British submariners of the war. His tally of 90,000 tons (91,440 tonnes) and a destroyer won him a posthumous Victoria Cross. Nevertheless, reinforcements from home waters kept up with the rate of losses, as British submarine building was at its zenith at this time.

Sicily to the end of the war in the Mediterranean

With the destruction of the Axis in North Africa, the Mediterranean central zone fell into total Allied control for the first time in the war. Convoys could now be routed through the Suez Canal, easing the supply chain to the Far East. This enabled the submarine force in the Mediterranean to prepare for Operation *Husky*, the invasion of Sicily. With the Axis in full retreat at sea, the submarines could fulfil a valuable strategic role as their primary task, while still attacking shipping.

On 10 July 1943, the largest amphibious operation undertaken up to that date was launched upon Sicily. The majority of the combined Allied submarine force supported the landings. The role of submarines in this operation took several guises. One, which had been going on for several weeks preceding the landings, was the reconnaissance and survey of the landing area. This often involved not only survey by periscope, but also the landing of engineers to test the softness of sand, gradient of beach, location of obstacles etc. As with Operation *Torch*, the submarines were additionally used as beacons to guide the landing craft to the right beach objectives.

Such was the domination of the sea by Allied submarines at this time, that they not only accomplished the tasks required for *Husky*, but they also increased the rate of sinkings of Axis shipping. In July three Italian submarines were sunk, along with some smaller naval craft and seven merchant ships.

After the capture of Sicily, the British submarine presence in the Mediterranean went into decline. Plans were already afoot to transfer some of the force to the Far East. In July, eight submarines were so moved. When Italy surrendered in September, the Algiers Flotilla was sent to the Far East. This left two small flotillas of submarines to mop up the remaining Axis shipping off France and in the Aegean.

From Operation *Husky* until the end of 1943, five British submarines were sunk. The submarine campaign in the Mediterranean effectively ended in October 1944. During the later phase, the submarines that took part were for the most part newer to the Mediterranean and were commanded by more recently commissioned officers. They proved ruthlessly successful in operation, sinking at least 53,000 tons (53,848 tonnes) of Axis shipping and several smaller naval vessels. Moreover, they subjected many shore-based targets to the deck gun. This level of success came at the loss of only one submarine – *Sickle* was mined off Livadia Island in the Greek Isles in June.

In January 1943, HMS *United* (*P44*) paid for sinking the destroyer *Bombardieri* by being hunted for 36 hours. Near to suffocation, many of the crew were sick when the hatch was finally opened to fresh air.

Looking at the Mediterranean campaign overall, some interesting points come to light. The Allies lost 49 submarines, of which around 23 were lost to surface forces, 21 to mines and one to a submarine. Aircraft sank possibly one at sea, and destroyed three in harbour at Malta. Loss statistics remain fluid, because so few of the wrecks have been found and large portions of the Axis anti-submarine records appear inaccurate or simply do not exist. Post-war research has added greater accuracy to some losses, especially where details of the locations of minefields have come to light, but the possibility of submarine accidents and unreported events cannot be ruled out. Nevertheless, some broad conclusions can be drawn.

The Axis is thought to have laid around 55,000 mines in the Mediterranean. The successes against Allied submarines by this effort made it certainly worthwhile. It compares very favourably with Allied mining statistics in home waters. Any comparison should be treated with caution, however, because there was comparatively little Axis submarine activity around British shores until late 1944.

The Italian surface forces claimed around 23 Allied submarines. Early on, some were caught on the surface. Hydrophone-equipped escorts sank eight, but the majority were hunted to destruction using Asdic and depth charges, with which the Italians became more expert as the war progressed. German units ably assisted them later.

While Allied submarines sank 19 Axis submarines, the Axis U-boats sank only one Allied submarine. All of the Axis submarines sunk were torpedoed while running on the surface, mostly in daylight. The way in which British submarines were operated in this theatre explains why the losses were so different.

British submarine strategy and tactics in the Mediterranean had some fairly unique features. The enemy was mostly faced by convoys with superior numbers of escorts and air support. The aggressive tactics favoured by U-boats in the Atlantic or US submarines in the Pacific, where the submarine was virtually treated as a torpedo boat with limited diving capability, could have proven fatal in the confined waters of the Mediterranean.

Instead, British submarines adopted a stealth approach. They remained submerged in daylight, not only in the patrol zones, but also in transit, accepting the limits this placed on latitude of action. The radio was used as sparingly as possible because of the accurate Axis radio direction finding stations and submarines were urged to remain undetected and unseen at all times. The clear waters of this theatre were especially

After transferring from the Mediterranean, HMS *Taurus* made an immediate impact in the Far East by sinking a Japanese submarine. British submarines grew in strength and confidence from this point on.

dangerous, as submarines could be spotted from the air even when submerged. So a 'porpoising' strategy was said to have been developed, whereby every quarter of an hour the submarine came up for an all-round view (especially for aircraft) through the periscope before submerging into the depths again. British submarines in the Mediterranean were initially painted dark blue to camouflage them when submerged. This had a bad side effect – they were more visible at night.

The successful T-Class HMS *Turbulent* was lost with all hands in March 1943, the dead including its famous commander J. W. 'Tubby' Linton, VC. Note the aft-pointing external tube behind the conning tower.

The British tactics worked because the distances from base to patrol area were relatively short and choke points along shipping lanes relatively common. Hence over two-thirds of attacks carried out by British submarines were in daylight while submerged. It was an unconventional, but a winning, strategy.

For three years, the Mediterranean was the most important and biggest theatre of British submarine operations. Just over 100 British submarines were sent there and 24 submarines of other Allied nations supported them. Although aircraft ended up sinking more of the Italy–North Africa supply ships towards the end of the campaign, they did this when Malta was secured. It was the submarines that continually harassed shipping throughout the campaign; hence, by its end, British and Allied submarines had sunk around half of the Axis losses in the Mediterranean. This figure could have been higher if submarines had not been diverted from the main strategy to deliver supplies and carry out clandestine operations.

THE FAR EAST

Outbreak of war with Japan to 1943
British submarines had been stationed in the Far East during the inter-war years as a countermeasure to possible Japanese aggression against British interests in the region. After the 1922 Naval Agreement, neither the United States nor Britain had enough capital ships to station a squadron nearby, so submarines and lighter forces had to suffice. The entire British submarine presence in the Far East had been withdrawn by July 1940. This ironically coincided with a cooling of diplomatic relations with Japan. While Britain was able to reinforce its defences in some areas with troops from India and Australia, there was not any realistic possibility of sending out any submarines because of the heavy demand on them in the home waters and the Mediterranean.

Until late 1943, Britain's submarine presence in the region was negligible, with only *Truant*, *Trusty* and *Trident* making brief appearances.

The Far East in 1943 to March 1945
In August 1943, the Admiralty had sent five submarines to the Far East. The first, *Templar*, arrived in Colombo in late September, followed by *Tactician*, *Taurus*, *Tally-Ho* and *Trespasser*. *Adamant* also returned and C-in-C Eastern Fleet moved to Colombo as well, forming the Fourth Flotilla. Finally, a genuine and lasting presence by the British submarine service had been established.

The major area of operations for the Fourth Flotilla remained the Malacca Straits. Reconnaissance was of key importance, as was the

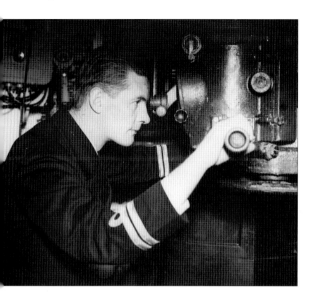

Lt Cdr L. W. A. Bennington, DSO*, DSC (the asterisk indicates that a bar was conferred), achieved notable successes in command of HMS *Porpoise* and *Tally-Ho*. His final account listed a light cruiser, a destroyer and a U-boat alongside over 20,000 tons (20,320 tonnes) of Axis shipping.

HMS *Tally-Ho* bears the scars of a scrape with a Japanese torpedo boat. It had already sunk the light cruiser *Kuma* by this time and was one of the leading submarines in the Far East campaign.

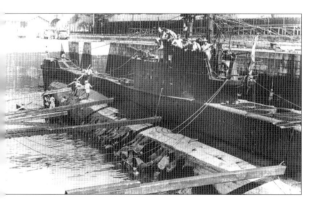

interdiction of supply shipping to Burma. Patrols were also to take place off Penang, because apart from the Japanese submarines, U-boats had begun to menace the area. The first success on patrol fell to *Tally-Ho*, which sank a small tanker in November, although defective torpedoes dogged this patrol. However, the major success of this period went to *Taurus*, which sank the large Japanese submarine *I34* outside Penang in November and later fought a gun duel with a sub-chaser before being forced to dive by aircraft.

By the end of 1943, British submarines had made their mark in the Far East and began to set up a permanent presence off the enemy's coast. Inauspicious it may have been, but it was far more successful than anything that had gone before.

By January 1944, the Eastern Fleet had been rebuilt around three heavy warships and two aircraft carriers and the force had moved, with the Fourth Flotilla, to Trincomalee. The depot ship *Maidstone* was on its way, along with six more submarines: *Stonehenge, Truculent, Sea Rover, Surf, Tantivy* and *Storm*. The year got off to a very good start. On 11 January, *Tally-Ho* was patrolling off Penang when it came across the light cruiser *Kuma*, escorted by a destroyer. *Tally-Ho*, which was commanded by one of the best shots in the submarine service, Lt Cdr L. W. A. Bennington, DSO, DSC, closed to 1,900 yards (1,737m) and fired seven torpedoes, gaining two hits and sending *Kuma* to the bottom. In only 15 fathoms of water, *Tally-Ho* made good its escape, despite having been bombed and depth charged.

Sadly, in March, the British lost their first submarine in the Far East theatre when *Stonehenge* failed to return from patrol. Its loss has never been explained and no evidence can be found to account for it. It is thought to lie off the north coast of Sumatra. A diving accident, collision or mine would seem the most likely cause.

Maidstone arrived in March and established the Eighth Flotilla, comprising the S-boats, while *Adamant* retained the T-boats as the Fourth Flotilla. Sinkings continued in April, by gun and torpedo. Of note was the rescue of an American airman from USS *Saratoga* (briefly under British command) off Sabang while under fire from shore batteries and in view of a Japanese torpedo boat. For this exploit, Lt Cdr Collet of *Tactician* received the American Legion of Merit.

In May, the Admiralty authorized the sinking of small vessels and junks. Every patrol now had the possibility of gun action against targets not worth a torpedo. Also submarine strength was increasing with the arrival of new S- and T-Class submarines and the older *Clyde, Severn* and *Porpoise*.

The continuing presence of submarines in the Malacca Straits and off Penang was yielding good results and consideration was now given to spreading the area of operations. Therefore, with the arrival of a third depot ship, *Wolfe*, the now 27-strong submarine force was divided into three flotillas, with the Second Flotilla being formed around *Wolfe*. The Eighth Flotilla was moved to Fremantle in Australia and came under overall command of the American Seventh Fleet. With it went *Telemachus*, *Tantivy*, *Tantalus*, *Spiteful*, *Sea Rover*, *Sturdy*, *Stoic*, *Sirdar*, *Storm* and the Dutch *O19* and T-Class *Zwaardvisch* (ex-*Talent*).

By the end of October 1944, the British submarines were becoming a thorn in the Japanese side. They had, by that date, sunk a cruiser, three submarines, six smaller naval vessels, 40,000 tons (40,060 tonnes) of merchant ships and nearly 100 smaller vessels. On top of this, 32 special operations had been launched, a bridge blown up, two aircrew rescued and nine shore installations shelled.

The Eighth Flotilla was used to sink ships in the Java Sea and surrounding areas. This relatively shallow stretch of water was difficult for the larger American submarines to operate safely in and became the zone of British operations. The fact remained that, so successful had the American submarine campaign against Japan been, targets of any size or import were becoming ever more difficult to find. Nevertheless, the British made an impact when they could locate the enemy.

The two Ceylon-based flotillas were also finding targets difficult to locate. From October 1944 to March 1945, the most important targets sunk were those destroyed in a chariot operation launched by *Trenchant* in Phuket harbour. A chariot operation comprised a two-man rideable torpedo, launched from a submarine, which was ridden to an enemy ship, where a limpet mine would be attached to the hull. They were generally considered too dangerous to undertake, but in this instance it was a success, with one ship sunk and one heavily damaged.

On 13 January, a strong anti-submarine force in the southern Malacca Straits detected *Strongbow*. The depth-charge attack that followed is considered to be one of the most violent and sustained attacks from which any British submarine was lucky enough to escape. In relatively shallow water, the submarine was extremely fortunate not to have been lost. Damaged and bottomed, *Strongbow* survived the attack, but the damage sustained was so extensive that it had to return to Trincomalee and then to Britain for repair. *Strongbow* was built with an all-welded pressure hull. It is interesting to speculate whether this innovation is what saved it from destruction.

Around the same time, Britain lost its last submarine of the war when the veteran *Porpoise* failed to return from patrol. It had been sent to the Penang area to lay mines and reported so doing on 9 January. Nothing more was ever heard from the vessel. At the time it was thought that it was probably sunk by the anti-submarine force that attacked *Strongbow*. It has also been suggested it was sunk by a Japanese aircraft. Post-war research shows there is nothing in the Japanese records to support either contention. The most likely explanation was that *Porpoise* either succumbed to a diving accident or was mined. It had laid a minefield off Penang in December and the Japanese had also mined the area.

By March 1945 the Malacca Straits were totally in the command of the submarines, and supply traffic through this area, even by junk, had virtually stopped. The Japanese Army in Burma was brought to star-vation by the success of the submarines in this area.

The final assault on Japan

In April, the British submarine force was readjusted. The Fourth Flotilla went to Fremantle and the Eighth moved to Subic Bay in the Philippines. There were now 38 operational British and Dutch submarines in theatre, with another five on their way out. The Fourteenth Flotilla, made up of XE-Craft (small submarines designed for special missions), had arrived.

Targets remained as scarce as ever, with most of the action taking place against smaller targets by gunfire. No fewer than 150 small vessels were sunk this way, up to the surrender of Japan in August. However, the submarines were to have one last major success and so were the XE-Craft.

On 8 June *Trenchant*, under Cdr A. R. Hezlet, was confronted with a major prize. It spotted the cruiser *Ashigara* and worked up an attack at the range of 4,800 yards (4,387m). A full spread of eight torpedoes was fired and, remarkably, five hit home. The cruiser settled and *Trenchant* turned to fire the stern torpedoes. These missed, but it did not matter as shortly thereafter the cruiser rolled over and sank, taking 800 crew with her. This sinking helped to make up for so many fruitless patrols by British submarines in the region.

The XE-Craft of the Fourteenth Flotilla were used on a daring raid into Singapore, where charges laid by *XE1* and *XE3* sank the cruiser *Takao*. *XE4* and *XE5* were used to cut the telephone cables between Saigon, Hong Kong and Singapore.

On 9 August, *Statesman* left Trincomalee for a patrol, indicative of this period of the war. It sank five junks by gunfire and finished off a derelict with torpedoes. In so doing it fired the last torpedo launched by a British submarine in World War II.

The British submarine campaign in the Far East had been completed with the loss of only three boats. This is a remarkably low figure given the shallow waters navigated during many of the operations. The force had only reached a critical size late in the war, when the American Navy had destroyed much of the Japanese merchant marine. Nevertheless, British submarines performed well. Their major success was undoubtedly closing the Malacca Straits and the port of Rangoon, thereby denuding the Japanese Army in Burma of supplies.

ROYAL NAVY SUBMARINE LOSSES

Fates of the S-Class boats

Seahorse	December 1939: probably mined in the Heligoland Bight
Starfish	9 January 1940: attacked by German surface forces and scuttled off Heligoland
Sterlet	18 April 1940: probably sunk by German surface forces in the Skagerrak
Shark	6 July 1940: attacked by aircraft off Skudenses and scuttled
Salmon	9 July 1940 (approx.): mined off Norway
Spearfish	1 August 1940: torpedoed in the North Sea by *U34*
Swordfish	7 November 1940: mined off the Isle of Wight
Snapper	11 February 1941: sunk by German surface forces off Ushant
P222	12 December 1942: sunk by Italian surface forces off Naples
Splendid	21 April 1943: attacked by German surface forces and scuttled off Corsica
Sahib	24 April 1943: attacked by Italian surface forces and scuttled off Sicily
Saracen	14 August 1943: attacked by Italian surface forces and scuttled off Bastia
Simoom	November 1943: mined in the Aegean
Stonehenge	March 1944: unknown loss north of Sumatra
Syrtis	28 March 1944: mined off Bodo
Sickle	June 1944: probably mined east of Levithia
Stratagem	22 November 1944: sunk by Japanese surface forces off Malacca

Fates of the T-Class boats

Tarpon	10 April 1940: sunk by German surface forces off Norway
Thistle	10 April 1940: sunk by German submarine *U4* off Skudenses
Triad	15 October 1940: sunk by the Italian submarine *Enrico Toti* off Cape Colonne
Triton	18 December 1940: sunk by Italian surface forces off Taranto
Tetrach	October 1941: mined off Sicily or Cavoli
Triumph	January 1942: probably mined off Cape Sounion
Tempest	13 February 1942: sunk by Italian surface forces off Taranto
Thorn	7 August 1942: sunk by Italian surface forces off Tobruk
Talisman	17 September 1942: mined off Sicily
Traveller	4 December 1942: probably mined off Taranto
P311	January 1943: probably mined off Maddalena
Tigris	27 February 1943: sunk by German surface forces off Naples
Turbulent	March 1943: probably mined off Sardinia
Thetis/Thunderbolt	raised after 1939 accident, renamed and sunk by Italian surface forces off Messina Strait, 14 March 1943
Trooper	October 1943: unknown loss, probably mined in Aegean

Fates of the U-Class boats

Undine	7 January 1940: attacked by German surface forces and scuttled off Heligoland
Unity	29 April 1940: collision off the Tyne
Usk	April 1941: mined off Cape Bon
Undaunted	13 May 1941: mined off Tripoli
Umpire	19 July 1941: collision off the Wash
Union	20 July 1941: sunk by Italian surface forces off Pantellaria
P32	August 1941: mined off Tripoli
P33	18 August 1941: sunk by Italian surface forces off Pantellaria
P38	23 February 1942: sunk by Italian surface forces off Tripoli
P39	26 March 1942: sunk by enemy aircraft in Malta
P36	1 April 1942: sunk by enemy aircraft in Malta
Upholder	14 April 1942: sunk by Italian surface forces off Tripoli
Urge	28 April 1942: mined east of Malta
Unique	October 1942: loss unknown in the Atlantic
Unbeaten	11 November 1942: accidentally sunk by Allied aircraft in Biscay
Utmost	25 November 1942: sunk by Italian surface forces west of Sicily
P48	25 December 1942: sunk by Italian surface forces off Tunis
Vandal	24 February 1943: foundered due to unknown cause off the Clyde
Untamed/Vitality	30 May 1943: foundered off the Clyde, salvaged and refitted as *Vitality*, sold for scrap 1946
Usurper	3 October 1943: sunk by German surface forces off La Spezia

Fates of other classes

Oxley	10 September 1939: torpedoed in accident by *Triton* off Norway
Seal	5 May 1940: captured by German surface forces off the Skaw
Odin	14 June 1940: sunk by Italian surface forces off Taranto
Grampus	16 June 1940: sunk by Italian surface forces off Syracuse
Orpheus	19 June 1940: mined off Benghazi
Phoenix	16 July 1940: sunk by Italian surface forces off Augusta
Narwhal	23 July 1940: sunk by German aircraft in the North Sea
Thames	23 July 1940: mined off Stavangar
Oswald	1 August 1940: rammed by Italian surface forces off Cape Spartivento
Rainbow	4 October 1940: run down by an Italian steamship in the Gulf of Otranto
H49	18 October 1940: sunk by German surface forces off Holland
Regulus	December 1940: mined in the Adriatic
Cachalot	30 July 1941: rammed by Italian surface forces off Benghazi
H31	December 1941: unknown loss (mined?) Atlantic/Biscay
Perseus	6 December 1941: mined off Zakinthos
Pandora	1 April 1942: sunk by enemy aircraft at Malta, raised and scrapped
Olympus	8 May 1942: mined off Malta
P514	21 June 1942: rammed mistakenly by a minesweeper off Canada
Regent	18 April 1943: mined in the Southern Adriatic
P615	18 April 1943: sunk by U123 off Freetown
Parthian	August 1943: mined in the Adriatic
Porpoise	January 1945: unknown loss (mined?) off Penang

BIBLIOGRAPHY

Akermann, Paul, *Encyclopaedia of British Submarines 1901–1955*,
   Periscope Publishing (2002)
Allaway, Jim, *Hero of the* Upholder, Periscope Publishing (2004)
Blamey, Joel, *A Submariner's Story*, Periscope Publishing (2002)
Brown, D. K. (ed.), *The Design and Construction of British Warships*,
   Conway (1996)
Chapman, Paul, *Submarine* Torbay, Hale (1989)
Compton-Hall, Richard, *Submarines at War 1939–45*,
   Periscope Publishing (2004)
Coote, John, *Submariner*, Leo Cooper (1991)
Cowie, Capt J. S., *Mines, Minelayers and Minelaying*,
   Oxford University Press (1949)
Davies, Roy, Nautilus, *The Story of Man under the Sea*,
   BBC (1995)
Dickison, Arthur P., *Crash Dive, In Action with*
   HMS Safari *1942–43*, Sutton (1999)
Evans, A. S., *Beneath the Waves, A History of HM Submarine*
   Losses 1904–1971, William Kimber (1986)
Gray, Edwyn, *Few Survived, A History of Submarine Disasters*,
   Leo Cooper (1986)
Hart, Sydney, *Submarine* Upholder, Oldbourne (1960)
Hezlet, Vice Adm Sir Arthur, *British and Allied Submarine*
   Operations in World War Two, Royal Navy Submarine
   Museum (2001)
Hill, Roger, *Destroyer Captain*, Periscope Publishing (2004)
Jameson, Rear Adm Sir William, *Submariners VC*,
   Periscope Publishing (2004)
Jones, Geoffrey, *Submarines versus U-Boats*, William Kimber (1986)
Kemp, Paul J., *The T-Class Submarine, The Classic British Design*,
   Arms and Armour (1990)
Lipscomb, Cdr F. W., *The British Submarine*, A&C Black (1954)
Mars, Alastair, *HMS* Thule *Intercepts*, Elek (1956)
– *The Story of a Submarine*, Fredrick Muller, 1953
– *British Submarines at War 1939–45*, William Kimber (1971)
McCartney, Innes, *Lost Patrols, Submarine Wrecks of the English*
   Channel, Periscope Publishing (2003)
Rohwer, Jürgen, *Allied Submarine Attacks of World War Two*,
   Greenhill Books (1997)
Roskill, Capt S. W., *The War at Sea 1939–45*, HMSO (1961)
Simpson, Rear Adm G. W. G.,
   Periscope View, Macmillan (1972)
Trenowden, Ian, *The Hunting*
   Submarine, The Fighting Life of
   HMS Tally-Ho, Crecy (1974)
Wingate, John, *The Fighting Tenth*,
   The Tenth Submarine Flotilla and the
   Siege of Malta, Periscope Publishing
   (2003)
Young, Edward, *One of Our Submarines*,
   Rupert Hart-Davis (1962)

HMS *Strongbow* was badly depth-charged in the Malacca Straits in 1945 but did not sink. It was so badly damaged that it had to be written off. Of the new all-welded hull series, *Strongbow*'s extra toughness may have been its salvation.

COLOUR PLATE COMMENTARY

A: THE EVOLUTION OF THE T-CLASS SUBMARINE

1) HMS *Triton* Group I design as completed in 1935. *Triton* was the longest of this design, measuring 277ft (84.43m) in length, compared to the standard 275ft (83.82m). On 10 April 1940 *Triton* was among the first submarines to be able to take advantage of unrestricted submarine warfare during the Norway campaign and sank two freighters and an escort with a spread of six torpedoes.

2) HMS *Traveller* Group II design as completed in 1942. *Traveller* was one of only two submarines of this design to be fitted with the Admiralty-pattern engines. Sadly it was lost during Operation *Torch*, mined off Taranto.

3) HMS *Telemachus* Group III design as completed in 1943. *Telemachus* served in the Far East with the Eighth Flotilla under the overall command of the American Seventh Fleet. It was scrapped in 1961.

B: THE EVOLUTION OF THE S-CLASS SUBMARINE

1) HMS *Swordfish* Group I design as completed in 1932. *Swordfish* was one of the first S-Class submarines ordered in 1929.

2) HMS *Sealion* Group II design as completed in 1934. *Sealion*'s design benefited from the lessons learnt by the Group I design and was enhanced by a number of modifications, including two escape chambers, strengthened bulkheads, and a reduction in the number of ballast tanks.

3) HMS *Safari* Group III design as completed in 1942. *Safari* was responsible for the sinking of 11 ships between February and May 1943 under its charismatic commander Ben Bryant (who won a second bar to his DSO at this time) and his replacement Lt R. B. Lakin. This submarine was one of the most successful with gun as well as torpedo.

C: THE EVOLUTION OF THE U-CLASS SUBMARINE

1) HMS *Unity* Group I design as completed in 1938. *Unity* was among the first three of this design ordered in 1936, the only three to be ready for the war's outbreak. Its war career was short-lived as it suffered a collision off the Tyne on 29 April 1940.

2) HMS *Upholder* Group II design as completed in 1940. On 25 April 1941, *Upholder*, under the leadership of Lt Cdr M. D. Wanklyn, sank a 5,400-ton (5,468-tonne) freighter off Tunisia. Two more were sunk on 1 May, adding 9,300 tons

The large pre-war minelayer HMS *Porpoise* had a successful career in all three theatres until January 1945, when it became the last British submarine sunk in action.

(9,449 tonnes) to *Upholder*'s tonnage tally. Its successes continued on the 24th when, partially damaged after a depth-charge attack on the 20th had knocked out its Asdic set, it made a dusk approach on a heavily escorted convoy and put its last two torpedoes into the 17,880-ton (18,166-tonne) troopship *Conte Rosso*, which sank with the loss of over 1,500 Italian troops. *Upholder* subsequently survived a heavy counter-attack of over 40 depth charges. *Upholder*'s run of successes against freighters, troopships and naval vessels, won Wanklyn the Victoria Cross. It is difficult to conceive of one more deserved. The citation made special note of the attack on *Conte Rosso*, which was carried out inside the escort screen without Asdic and in failing light, making the spotting of the escort ships very difficult. This exceptional submarine commander was already the recipient of the DSO. *Upholder* was sunk by Italian surface forces off Tripoli on 14 April 1942.

Cdr A. R. Hezlet DSO* receiving the American Legion of Merit for sinking the Japanese heavy cruiser *Ashigara*. This significant success made up for the general paucity of targets in the latter stages of the Far East campaign.

46

LEFT **Lt Cdr E. P. Young, DSO, became the first Royal Naval Volunteer Reserve (RNVR) officer to command a Royal Navy submarine when commissioned to HMS *Storm*. He had an outstanding career. After the war he wrote *One of Our Submarines* about his experiences. It is widely regarded as the finest book of its genre.**

3) HMS *Venturer* Group III design as completed in 1943. She became the first submarine in history to sink another submarine while both were submerged. The hydrophone played a key role. The difficulty with such an attack is to judge the depth of the target. From the noise it was making the U-boat was probably using its *Schnorchel* (snorkel) to transit submerged. The torpedoes fired were set to 30 and 36ft (9.1 and 11m) and one hit resulted. The unlucky target was *U864*.

D: GROUP III DESIGN, T-CLASS SUBMARINE OF 1944

The classic type III T-Class design is depicted here. This is widely considered to be the finest British submarine design of the war.

E: OTHER SUBMARINE DESIGNS THAT FOUGHT IN WORLD WAR II

1) HMS *Seal*, a minelayer, as completed in 1939. This was among the five minelayers in the Grampus-Class that were built before the outbreak of hostilities.

2) HMS *Olympus* of the O-Class, as completed in 1930. *Olympus* formed part of the First Submarine Flotilla during the campaign in the Mediterranean. It was damaged by a bomb while in dry-dock in Malta and eventually sank due to a mine off Malta on 8 May 1942.

3) HMS *Rover* of the R-Class, as completed in 1931. *Rover* was the only British submarine in the Far East at the outbreak of war with Japan. It was undergoing a major repair programme in Singapore, having been damaged in the Mediterranean, and eventually it was towed to Bombay for completion of these repairs. *Rover* was scrapped in 1946.

F: *SAFARI* ATTACKS COASTAL SHIPPING

Safari was one of the more successful submarines of World War II and played a crucial role during the war in the Mediterranean, where the British strategy of intercepting the supply lines for the Axis forces resulted in over 47 merchant vessels and many smaller craft of various sizes being sunk. *Safari* was eventually sold for scrap in 1946, but sank on tow; the wreck is now privately owned.

G: U-CLASS RETURNS TO MALTA

The U-Class submarine will always be associated with the war in the Mediterranean, the siege of Malta and with the Royal Navy's most successful submarine captain, Lt Cdr M. D. Wanklyn, VC, DSO. The U-Class vessels arrived at Malta during the first few months of 1941 and were used primarily to patrol the Tunisian coast. However, shortly after their arrival they launched a number of extremely successful attacks against Italian ships and submarines, opening up the North African supply routes to the British forces. Most famous during this campaign are the exploits of the Fighting Tenth (the Tenth Flotilla) formed from these Malta submarines.

BELOW **Cdr Ben Bryant DSO** (foreground). In command of HMS *Safari*, his extensive use of the deck gun was notable, as is his claim to have sunken a tank on Ras Ali pier by torpedo – a unique achievement. Bryant went on to become a successful flotilla commander in 1943.**

INDEX

References to illustrations are shown in **bold**. Plates are shown with page and caption locators in brackets.